D1367625

NEW STUDIES IN ETHICS

HEGELIAN ETHICS

Hegelian Ethics

W. H. WALSH

Professor of Logic and Metaphysics, University of Edinburgh

MACMILLAN
London · Melbourne · Toronto
ST MARTIN'S PRESS
New York
1969

Published by
MACMILLAN AND CO LTD
Little Essex Street London WC2
and also at Bombay Calcutta and Madras
Macmillan South Africa (Publishers) Pty Ltd Johannesburg
The Macmillan Company of Australia Pty Ltd Melbourne
The Macmillan Company of Canada Ltd Toronto
St Martin's Press Inc New York

Library of Congress catalog card no. 69–13686

Printed in Great Britain by
Richard Clay (The Chaucer Press) Ltd
Bungay Suffolk

CONTENTS

CONTENTS

EDITOR'S PREFACE

Hegel has been neglected – by British philosophers at any rate – for more than a generation. Part of the reason for this is undoubtedly his notoriously difficult style of writing. Professor Walsh at one point in this study says, 'If only he could have matched the vigour of his thought with skill in self-expression . . .'; and all who have laboured to understand Hegel must have wished at many points that he could have done so. Another reason for Hegel's unpopularity, so far as moral philosophy is concerned at least, is the widespread belief that the most repugnant forms of totalitarianism from which our modern world has suffered, and still suffers, owe their inspiration to him.

Professor Walsh's monograph reintroduces Hegelian ethics to us. With great skill he redeems the vigour of Hegel's thought from the obscurities of its original expression and brings out its main lines very clearly. He also rescues Hegel's view that morality is primarily a social rather than a personal phenomenon from misunderstanding. Showing Hegel's debt to, and divergences from, Kant, he presents an exposition of the former's ethic which is sympathetic but not uncritical.

All students of moral philosophy, and indeed all readers who are interested in ideas which have gone to the shaping of our world, will be grateful for this careful analysis and critique of a thinker whose ethical reflections were original and influential.

University of Exeter   W. D. HUDSON

PREFACE

I am grateful to my colleague Professor H. B. Acton for commenting on this essay in typescript, as well as for discussing with me many of the main points of the subject. I should also like to record that I could not have attempted to write about Hegel's ethics even at this length, were it not for the existence of Sir Malcolm Knox's translations, with their admirable explanatory notes.

W. H. W.

I. INTRODUCTION

Georg Wilhelm Friedrich Hegel was born in 1770 at Stuttgart, which was then the capital of the Duchy of Würtemberg. His father was an official in the Duke's service. Hegel received his basic education at the local grammar school and then went on to study philosophy and theology at Tübingen, where the poet Hölderlin and the precocious philosopher Schelling were his closest friends. The institution they attended was a seminary for intending pastors in the Lutheran Church, but Hegel seems to have had no serious thoughts of entering the ministry. On leaving Tübingen in 1793 he spent several years working as a private tutor, first at Bern in Switzerland and later at Frankfurt. A small legacy he received on the death of his father in 1799 enabled him to give up this work, and in 1801 he became a Privat-dozent teaching philosophy at the University of Jena. Hegel stayed at Jena until 1807, when the university was closed by the invading French forces. After eighteen months as editor of a local newspaper in Bamberg, Hegel was appointed headmaster of a grammar school in Nuremberg. He held this position for eight years, teaching his pupils philosophy as well as classics and mathematics, and writing his formidable *Science of Logic* in his spare time. It was not until he was forty-six, in 1816, that he held a regular professorship in a university. He went in that year to be professor of philosophy at Heidelberg; two years later he left Heidelberg to become professor in the recently founded University of Berlin. Hegel was still professor of philosophy at Berlin when he died in a cholera epidemic in 1831.

Hegel is often thought of as a Prussian apologist, but in fact he was a south German who spent most of his life in that part of the country, and only one of his major works was written during his Berlin period. The *Phenomenology of Mind* was composed at Jena and, notoriously, finished on the eve of Napoleon's victory there;

the *Science of Logic*, as already stated, was produced while Hegel was a headmaster; the *Encyclopaedia of the Philosophical Sciences* appeared in its original form as a handbook to Hegel's lectures at Heidelberg. As for the *Philosophy of Right*, which came out at Berlin in 1821, many of the doctrines it contains had already been outlined in the corresponding sections of the *Encyclopaedia*, and some of the most striking among them are to be found in the essay on natural law Hegel published in 1802 and in the incomplete 'System of Ethics' on which he was working in his early years at Jena. Hegel's bad reputation as a time-server springs mainly from the harsh things he has to say about his contemporaries in the preface to the *Philosophy of Right* and from his insistence there (Knox translation, p. 10) that

since philosophy is the exploration of the rational, it is for that very reason the apprehension of the present and the actual, not the erection of a beyond, supposed to exist, God knows where, or rather which exists, and we can perfectly well say where, namely in the error of a one-sided, empty, ratiocination.

It looks from this as if Hegel thought it the business of philosophy to justify existing institutions, and this impression is supported by the fact that he denounces by name his predecessor at Heidelberg, J. F. Fries, who was suspended from his chair at Jena after taking part in the Wartburg Students' Festival in 1817. In fact, however, Hegel's quarrel with Fries was not so much over his opposition to established authority as for the emphasis he placed on unin-structed public opinion; it was Fries' appeal to personal con-viction that Hegel challenged. Fries thought that political initiative should all come from below, i.e. from the people; to Hegel this was dangerous irrationalism. It is not self-evident that Fries was right in this controversy. Nor is it true to say that Hegel believed that philosophy must justify existing institutions; as will become clear, he thought it should neither justify nor condemn but simply characterise and explain.

In general, Hegel was not a political reactionary but a moderate constitutionalist. The French Revolution broke out in his student days, and made a lasting impression on him. It seemed to Hegel that the Revolution had completed a process begun at the

Reformation, a process which was in essentials one of liberation. But though Hegel emphasised that in this process men had increased their powers of self-determination, he was anxious to add that this did not mean that henceforth all would be given over to individual caprice. On the contrary, men were now more free because their lives were now more rationally governed. The most important thing about the French Revolution on this way of looking at it was its emphasis on the rule of law. Hegel thought of the rule of law as lying at the centre of modern political life, and as excluding personal despotism and mob democracy alike.

Hegel had a remarkable intellectual range, as reflection on the subject-matter of his books and posthumously published lectures will show. He had studied the world of classical antiquity profoundly, and was as familiar with Greek art and Roman law as with Greek and Latin literature and the philosophies of Plato and Aristotle. He had a continuing if not very sympathetic interest in the ancient Jews, dating back to his student days, and knew something of the cultures of India and China. The Middle Ages were largely foreign to him, but the Protestant mystics were not, and his thought was considerably influenced by their writings. Among his literary contemporaries he knew and admired Goethe as well as Hölderlin. Hegel deepened his knowledge of his own time by studying the political economists; he was also a regular reader of the English Press. In addition he kept up, or aspired to keep up, an interest in scientific developments; it was on a scientific subject that he presented a dissertation when seeking the right to lecture at Jena. The dissertation is remembered today for what is supposed to be a monumental error on Hegel's part, in denying on *a priori* grounds the possibility of any planet between Mars and Jupiter. It is not clear that he fell into the error, but in any case, as Walter Kaufmann has remarked, the interesting thing about the whole episode is that Hegel should have had the competence to write an acceptable dissertation on that sort of subject at all.

Hegel had few immediate disciples of note in Germany, apart from the 'Left' Hegelians, David Strauss, Ludwig Feuerbach and Karl Marx. Outside Germany it was a long time before he was appreciated, doubtless because of the difficulties of his thought and his rebarbative style of writing. His influence was not felt in Italy until the end of the nineteenth century; in France he made little or no impact until shortly before 1939. But the situation was different in Britain, where there was a flourishing school of Hegelians as early as 1870. There were also American Hegelians of some consequence from 1880 onwards.

Of the British Hegelians referred to below, Thomas Hill Green (1836–82) is perhaps the most interesting on personal grounds. The son of a Church of England clergyman, Green went to Oxford in the middle 1850s and soon became known for his radical political views as well as for his philosophical seriousness. He was a keen defender of the foreign policy of Cobden and Bright against that of Palmerston, and later a passionate supporter of the cause of the North in the American Civil War. Elected a Fellow of Balliol College in 1860, Green spent the rest of his life teaching in Oxford, becoming professor of moral philosophy in the university in 1878. But he combined his teaching with many practical interests, serving, for example, on a commission on school education in the English Midlands in the 1860s and on the Oxford Town Council in the 1870s. He was also active in national politics as a member of the Liberal Party, as well as in the Temperance movement. Green's major work *Prolegomena to Ethics* was not quite complete at the time of his premature death, and was published in the following year by his literary executors.

Francis Herbert Bradley (1846–1924) was one of a group of young Oxford philosophers who admired Green, but was in many ways a very different character. To begin with, ill health made him a recluse instead of an active member of society: his whole life was spent holding a fellowship which involved no teaching duties and left him free to devote himself to philosophy. But there were differences of temperament too. Where Green was radical and forward-looking, Bradley was continually suspicious of the ideas of what he called 'advanced thinkers': he saw it as a major task for himself to expose their pretensions and superficiality. And he entered on the work with genuine passion as well as with formidable literary and dialectical equipment: he both

4

believed in the cause and delighted in the controversy. Bradley's controversial powers were at their height in his first two books, *Ethical Studies* and *The Principles of Logic*. His most ambitious work, *Appearance and Reality*, an essay in metaphysics, is more measured and perhaps for that reason less successful: it reveals less of his mind. It was a mind which, despite Bradley's own theories, was highly individual: at once acute and prejudiced, penetrating and perverse. One can scarcely think that he and Green could ever have been close friends.

Bernard Bosanquet (1848–1923) spent only a small part of his life as a teacher of philosophy, though he produced a large number of works on the subject, the best known being his *Logic* (1888), *History of Aesthetic* (1892), *Philosophical Theory of the State* (1899) and *The Principle of Individuality and Value* (1912). Like Green, Bosanquet held that there should be no divorce between theory and practice, but that the two should continually enrich each other. Bosanquet found his own practical outlet in social work, particularly on behalf of the Charity Organisation Society in London, in which his future wife Helen Dendy was also active. In 1909 Mrs Bosanquet was a member of the Royal Commission on the Poor Law and supported the principle of moral reform against the principle of state interference successfully pressed by Beatrice Webb. There is no reason to suppose that Bosanquet took a different view from his wife on this matter. A middle-of-the-road man, who believed in the meeting of extremes in contemporary philosophy, he was, like others of his kind, altogether less radical than he thought.

II. THE TASKS OF ETHICS

Very few students of philosophy in the English-speaking world today have an accurate knowledge of even the main outlines of Hegel's ethical theories, and this fact renders profitable discussion of these theories extremely difficult. It happens, however, that in his ethical thinking Hegel was continuously preoccupied with the views of Kant; the question what Kant got right in moral philosophy and just where he went wrong is one to which he returns again and again. To call Hegel a Kantian in his general philosophical outlook would certainly be mistaken: his implacable hostility to the whole Kantian enterprise of drawing a limit to the powers of reason precludes our taking that designation seriously. But to call him a Kantian in ethics, though of course a Kantian with a difference, is not altogether far-fetched. I therefore propose to introduce Hegelian ethics by means of a comparison with the parallel doctrines in Kant, doctrines which I can perhaps assume to be generally familiar to the reader.

Let me start with a point over which the two thinkers ostensibly diverge very sharply: the question of the task, or tasks, of the moral philosopher. Kant in the preface to the *Groundwork* said that his 'sole aim' was 'to seek out and establish the supreme principle of morality'.[1] In the first section of that work he went on to argue that, once what was involved in the notions of the good will and duty was taken into account, we could see that 'conformity of actions to universal law as such' should 'alone . . . serve the will as its principle'.[2] Hence the conclusion that 'I ought never to act except in such a way that I can also will that my maxim should become a universal law'.[3] This certainly sounds like a moral prescription, and is treated as such by Kant, as in the following passage:

Thus I need no far-reaching ingenuity to find out what I have to do in order to possess a good will. Inexperienced in the course of world

6

affairs and incapable of being prepared for all the chances that happen in it, I ask myself only 'Can you also will that your maxim should become a universal law?' Where you cannot, it is to be rejected.[4]

An ethics which professes to provide what Kant in the following paragraph calls 'this compass', by which 'human reason . . . is well able to distinguish, in all cases that present themselves, what is good or evil, right or wrong',[5] has every appearance of being normative as opposed to descriptive.

By contrast Hegel argued that it was not for the moral philosopher to give moral advice, even moral advice of a highly general kind. The philosopher's task was to understand the world, not to intervene in it. Understanding of this sort was certainly more than a matter of simple description: the facts under study had to be seen in their connections and the principle or principles which underlay them had to be made explicit. It remained true, none the less, that the role of the philosopher, in ethics as elsewhere, was very much a spectator's role. And Hegel argued in a celebrated discussion in the preface to the *Philosophy of Right* that no other role was open to him:

> One word more about giving instruction as to what the world ought to be. Philosophy in any case always comes on the scene too late to give it. As the thought of the world, it appears only when actuality is already there cut and dried after its process of formation has been completed. The teaching of the concept, which is also history's inescapable lesson, is that it is only when actuality is mature that the ideal first appears over against the real and that the ideal apprehends this same real world in its substance and builds it up for itself into the shape of an intellectual realm. When philosophy paints its grey in grey, then has a shape of life grown old. By philosophy's grey in grey it cannot be rejuvenated but only understood. The owl of Minerva spreads its wings only with the falling of the dusk.[6]

The precise reasoning behind this declaration is obscure, but presumably Hegel was relying here on an antithesis, familiar in the writings of other speculative philosophers of history, between ages of action and ages of reflection, creative periods in which men's achievements are arrived at unselfconsciously, and critical periods which take stock of what has been achieved and lay bare its theoretical foundations. Philosophy on this view belongs to the second type of period and can hence originate nothing but merely make us aware of what exists. According to Hegel, this is precisely what Plato did for the Greeks: his *Republic* gives expression to current thought about politics and is 'in essence nothing but an interpretation of the nature of Greek ethical life'.[7] To take it as 'an empty ideal' which contrasts with reality is, in Hegel's opinion, the height of superficiality.

We seem here to be faced with an absolute difference of view, but there are respects in which the difference is even so not complete. For one thing, Kant himself sometimes writes as if his aim, or at least part of his aim, were to make explicit a principle which, if I may so put it, is already embodied in actuality. Thus he says in the preface to the *Groundwork* that he will 'proceed analytically from common knowledge to the formulation of its supreme principle and then back again synthetically from an examination of this principle and its origins to the common knowledge in which we find its application';[8] if the meaning of the second part of this sentence is not obvious, the implications of its opening words are quite clear. And that Kant thought he had kept to his intentions here is shown by the remarks he makes at the very end of the second section of his work, where he sums up what has been done and is still to be done. He writes there that he has not proved that morality is 'no mere phantom of the brain',[9] but 'merely shown by developing the concept of morality generally in vogue that autonomy of the will is unavoidably bound up with it or rather is its very basis'.[10] In other words, he has laid bare the principle on which moral agents believe themselves to act, but produced no argument for the view that they are in fact in a position to act morally. The third part of the *Groundwork* is intended to remedy this deficiency. But the first two parts, in which Kant states the all-important doctrines of the categorical imperative and the autonomy of the will, are in Kant's own words 'merely analytic',[11] and as such are not unlike essays in the Hegelian style.

Nor does Hegel himself contrive to stick to his own programme with entire consistency. His aim in the *Philosophy of Right* was to seize on the essential nature of the modern ethical world, which meant disentangling and doing justice to various elements which are actually active in that world. Hegel would no doubt have insisted that his results, both in their general outline and in their details, were authentic just because they had their counterpart in the facts. Yet it remains true that the Hegelian procedure involved evaluation as well as description: there was, necessarily, an element of selection in it. We see this most clearly in the parts of Hegel's writings which modern readers find least edifying, the passages which speak with contempt of contemporary liberal movements and in which Hegel appears to be engaged in the unworthy task of finding philosophical justification for maintaining the *status quo*. But we also see it, more interestingly, in occasional essays such as those on the constitution of Würtemberg and the English Reform Bill, where Hegel appeals to philosophical principles to condemn existing states of affairs. A party in Würtemberg after the collapse of Napoleon wanted to restore the rights of the Estates as they had existed before the French Revolution; Hegel saw this as a reactionary step, intolerable because it meant that the country must rest content with particular privileges instead of being brought under the rule of universal law. A structure of this sort, the implication was, could not satisfy the demands of reason, and these demands had authority just because they had achieved recognition in the Revolution. Similarly in the essay on the English Reform Bill, written in the year of his death, we find Hegel surveying the British political scene with a disapproving eye and condemning the constitution as resting on an 'inherently disconnected aggregate of positive provisions'.[12] What the British lacked, and would continue to lack if the Bill were enacted, was a rational political and social structure; whether or not the arrangements under which their public life proceeded worked, they were such as no civilised observer could accept. In his account of modern society in the *Philosophy of Right* Hegel had drawn on his extensive knowledge of British conditions to a marked extent, above all in the prominence which he gave to 'civil society' as opposed to the family on the one hand and the state on the other. Britain was the country in which civil society, or the 'state external' as Hegel calls it,[13] was most clearly

9

distinguishable. But though he picked on this aspect of British life as belonging to the essence of the modern world, Hegel felt no qualms about rejecting other aspects of it as outmoded and untypical. And in so doing he revealed that his depiction of 'the actual' in politics and morals was far from being a matter of simple description.

Despite these similarities, the reader may still feel that there is a major difference in tone between Hegel's ethics and Kant's, and that this connects with their differing views on the tasks of moral philosophy. I think myself that this feeling is justified. Kant, even if we take him as occupied in rendering explicit what is already present in the common moral consciousness, is far from being a neutral commentator on the ethical scene. When he denounces an ethical theory such as Utilitarianism or Moral Sense as heteronomous, his aim is to expose more than intellectual error. Theories of this sort lead to positive immorality as well as to mental confusion; it is important to root them out because of their corrupting influence. Kant thus regards autonomy of the will as a requirement which is not only accepted by the common moral consciousness but must be so accepted; what purported to be a moral system, but was based on some other principle, for example on the ascription of moral authority to some institution or to some person other than the agent, would simply not deserve the name. Kant made some references, especially in his *Religion within the Bounds of Mere Reason*,[14] to circumstances in which these conditions obtained, but was not in general very curious about them: whether they were found among the remote Siberians or among modern Europeans, his tendency was simply to dismiss them as primitive. By contrast Hegel had a far more historical outlook, and with it some appreciation of the varieties of the moral life. True, he began as an avid reader of Kant's book on religion, and took over many of Kant's prejudices in his early writings; this accounts, among other things, for the hostile picture we find there of the moral life of the ancient Jews, and for the presentation of Jesus as a moral reformer who sought to rescue Jewish life from a spiritless conformism. But in later years he saw quite clearly that it was anachronistic to look at the ethical world of

Greek tragedy through modern eyes, taking Antigone as moved by conscientious scruples and Creon as riding roughshod over them. The importance of the individual moral agent and his right to free decision had simply not been recognised at this time. The 'principle of self-subsistent particularity' [15] was beginning to break through in Plato's day, but it was not until the Christian era that it really established itself. 'It is historically subsequent to the Greek world, and the philosophical reflection which descends to its depth is likewise subsequent to the substantial Idea of Greek philosophy.' [16] In other words, we must not look to the Greeks for moral life as we know it, nor to Greek ethical reflection for anything like a full account of that life.

The logical conclusion of this historical approach must be some form of ethical relativism, or perhaps the dissolution of ethics in sociology. That Hegel reached neither conclusion explicitly is to be explained partly by his failure to appreciate the radical implications of his own procedure, partly by his retention of the notion of moral progress, which enabled him in his mature thought to see the modern world as not only different from the ancient but also superior to it. Yet the lesson of his own thinking should have been only that there is no putting the clock back in morals. It is, for example, unthinkable on Hegel's assumptions that a modern society should dispense with the principle of subjective freedom, and any project to do so can be dismissed as wholly absurd. Its absurdity will, however, not be what Kant would have said it was, namely moral absurdity; it would arise rather from its being historically incongruous. Thus all Hegel could properly find to say against a moral system which diverged markedly from that which prevailed in his own time would be that the ways of proceeding it advocated were impractical. If it turned out to be viable after all, Hegel would have no rational ground on which to object to it.

III. THE SCOPE OF ETHICS

I turn now to a second point of comparison between Hegel and Kant: over what might be called the scope of their ethical theories. In general, it would be true to say that Kant gave the term 'ethics' a restricted meaning; he took it to be concerned, in essentials, with the motives and intentions of individual moral agents. At the centre of morality there lay, for him, the concept of the good will, of the will, that is to say, which wills the action it judges to be right for itself alone, and not for any ulterior purpose. The will of the moral agent must be self-determining (an imposed or imitated morality is a contradiction in terms), and while a man cannot control what happens in the world, he has absolute power over his motives. The question whether an act has moral worth turns on this account on what went on in the mind of the agent concerned at the time he did the act; it is, first and foremost, a question which the agent has to answer for himself. It would, of course, be quite wrong to suggest that Kant's only interest in ethics was in the personal aspect of morality; he recognised clearly that ethics has an applied as well as a pure side, and explored this at length in his lectures on ethics and in the *Metaphysic of Morals*. It remains true, none the less, that being moral was for Kant primarily a matter of personal concern.

Now Hegel was ready to admit that morality involves personal choice and intention, but he gives this aspect of the situation a relatively minor place in his discussions of human conduct. The *Philosophy of Right* contains three main sections, labelled respectively 'Abstract Right', 'Morality' and 'Concrete Ethics', and the subject-matter of the second corresponds generally to that of Kant's ethics as just described. But whereas Kant dwells on these topics at length, Hegel dismisses them with comparative brevity: the section on morality occupies only about one-seventh of his book. And the subjects which make up the rest of the work seem on the face of it to have little to do with Kant's main interest. 'Abstract Right' is, in effect, a consideration of man in a number of elementary legal capacities: as the possessor of property, as a party to contracts, as liable to suffer damage, civil or criminal, at the hands of another. A recurring theme in Hegel's treatment is, admittedly, the increasing attention paid at the different levels to the claims of individual personality; in that way 'Abstract Right' is shown to point forward to 'Morality'. But much of the detail seems to be treated for its own sake, and the section as a whole belongs to philosophy of law rather than to ethics as commonly understood. Nor, despite its title, has the section on 'Concrete Ethics' much to do with the moral dilemmas of individuals. A large portion of it is devoted to an analysis of the main components of modern social life, the family, civil society and the state; perceptive and intelligent as this is, it explains the background of moral judgments rather than reflects on them directly. Hegel would no doubt argue, correctly, that anyone who attempted to depict moral life in the concrete and left these aspects out of account would present a one-sided and obviously incomplete view of the situation. But the fact is, even so, that his own interest in these topics is altogether greater than it would have been had he merely set out to improve on Kant. This is shown most clearly in the extent to which he enters on the discussion of points which belong not even to political philosophy but to practical politics: questions about the role of the monarch, the constitution and function of the Estates, the justification of trial by jury. If we can never quite forget that the person who engages in these discussions is a moral philosopher, the fact remains that his conception of the scope of moral philosophy is unusually wide.

How, if at all, could this attempt to shift the centre of interest in ethics from the personal to the social aspect be justified? Hegel's main reason for making it is undoubtedly that it represents a return to realism in the discussion of conduct. To lay exclusive emphasis on the personal side of action is to forget that an action is carried out in the public world, and is of interest for other reasons than that it embodies or fails to embody good will. Hegel concedes in his pedantic way that

13

the right of the subjective will is that whatever it is to recognise as valid shall be seen by it as good, and that an action, as its aim entering upon external objectivity, shall be imputed to it as right or wrong, good or evil, legal or illegal, in accordance with its *knowledge* of the worth which the action has in this objectivity.[17]

He allows, in other words, that it is a necessary condition of an act's being recognised as right or wrong that it should be the agent's own act. But he denies that choice and intention, or if we prefer it the right of free judgment, have more to do with morals than that. 'The right of giving recognition only to what my insight sees as rational is the highest right of the subject', yet 'owing to its subjective character it remains a formal right; against it the right which reason *qua* the objective possesses over the subject remains firmly established'.[18]

Hegel puts the same point a page or two later in a discussion of conscience. 'True conscience', he tells us, 'is the disposition to will what is absolutely good', and as such 'is a sanctuary which it would be sacrilege to violate'.[19] But this does not mean that we have to defer to the conscientious decisions of individuals in particular cases; it does not mean that the fact that an act proceeds from conscience is a sufficient condition of its being right. On the contrary:

What is right and obligatory is the absolutely rational element in the will's volitions and therefore it is not in essence the *particular* property of an individual, and its form is not that of feeling or any other private (i.e. sensuous) type of knowing, but essentially that of universals determined by thought, i.e. the form of laws and principles. Conscience is therefore subject to the judgment of its truth or falsity, and when it appeals only to itself for a decision, it is directly at variance with what it wishes to be, namely the rule for a mode of conduct which is rational, absolutely valid, and universal. For this reason the state cannot give recognition to conscience in its private form as subjective knowing, any more than science can grant validity to subjective opinion, dogmatism, and the appeal to a subjective opinion.[20]

It might be said in comment on this that, so far from disagreeing with Kant, it simply repeats an important part of his ethical theory. I must leave this question without discussion here. I should, however, like to take up the comparison which Hegel makes in the last sentence of the passage quoted, and to ask if he is correct in arguing that what was called above the right of free judgment is in exactly the same position in morals as it is in science. Whatever Kant's own view on this point, it seems clear that a number of subsequent philosophers, to say nothing of practical moralists, have been inclined to dispute the comparison. Morals, they suggest, is and must be more a matter of choice than, say, mathematics or history; it involves personal commitment in a way which Hegel plainly fails to appreciate.

If I am involved in working out a mathematical problem I must, no doubt, put myself into my work to the extent of seeing the connections between the different stages of the argument for myself; I must also be able to appreciate that the premises from which I argue are correct. But some of these premises will, generally, be given as true, while others will be the conclusions of theorems that have previously been proved. Furthermore, I shall conduct my argument according to certain logical principles (for example, the rule of *modus ponens*) whose validity I suppose myself justified in taking for granted. If I were a competent mathematician I could without great difficulty produce proofs for myself of the mathematical principles I use in my argument, and if I were a logician as well as a mathematician, as relatively few mathematicians are, I might even be able to offer a justification of the logical rules on which I rely, or at least of some of them. But I shall not normally be called upon to authenticate either. For the limited purposes which concern me I can take it that there is a publicly accredited body of mathematical and logical knowledge, and allow myself to draw on it without inspecting its credentials for myself. By taking advantage of what is generally conceded here I shall not be thought to be untrue to my profession as a thinker, or to have abandoned the right of free judgment in favour of an authority which is essentially alien. I am only recognising the simple fact that mathematics, like other branches of knowledge, represents a collective rather than an individual achievement, and that in this field, as in the world of learning generally, I have the good fortune to stand on the shoulders of others. Indeed, to insist on my right of free judgment against what is held to be true by well-qualified persons is, here at least, always presumptuous and often downright conceit. I *may* be right in challenging the authorities, but the chances are that I shall not.

The question now is whether the same sort of case could be made out about morals. And the commonest answer today is that it cannot. A person who possesses a skill must be able to operate according to the rules of his craft, but he can have taken over those rules from another, without subjecting them to any tests of his own. A thinker must be able to think for himself, but that does not mean that he must have personally authenticated every principle he uses in his thinking. But morals is not a matter of mere skill or of mere thinking: the moral agent manifests his will, and that fact introduces an element into the situation to which there is no counterpart in the other cases. We see this from the admission that it is no excuse in a moral situation for an agent to plead that the precepts to which he appealed were those he had been taught, or those which were accepted in the best circles known to him. That men commonly thought of as decent take something as morally correct in the end does nothing to commend it morally; attempted justification on these lines is simply out of place. A man must not only make his own moral judgments; he must also, in a sense, make his own moral principles. Or if that is going too far, he must at least commit himself to the principles to which he makes appeal, and be ready to defend their application if they are challenged. There is no point at which he can lean on the insights of another, or claim support from collective wisdom.

It is some such conviction as this which lies behind the view, widely shared today, that a man's morals are at bottom his own concern and nobody else's. We often hear it said, particularly by enlightened people, that they do not presume to judge for others; there are standards they try to observe in their own conduct, but these are chosen by themselves to apply only to themselves. If others choose to direct their lives by different principles, that is their own affair. Now it is not difficult to show that people who talk in this way do not entirely mean what they say. They will tolerate moral diversity of various kinds, but they will not allow absolutely anything to count as a morality, for example a state of affairs in which the agents see no virtue in sincerity or 'authenticity'. But there is a much more serious objection to the attitude than that. The real trouble with it is that it misconceives the whole institution of morality. Those who make moral principles a matter of choice in the way explained assimilate the moral life to the life of artistic expression and appreciation; they take it as if it were primarily of private concern. But the truth is rather that morality is first and foremost a social institution, performing a social role, and only secondarily, if at all, a field for individual self-expression. Morality is necessary to a community in the sort of way law is: both are devices for checking personal greed for the benefit of the common interest. And just as law in its fundamentals must be the same for all citizens, with nothing optional about it, so too must morality.

Now it could, of course, be argued that what has just been said, if true at all, applies only to a part of morality; in fact, to the part of it which is conventionally accepted and for that reason is at best of minor interest. Let it be agreed that social life would be impossible unless the members of society observed some restraints over and above those imposed on them by the legal system; unless, for example, they were prepared in some measure at least to carry out their undertakings and have regard to the rights and claims of others. It is not, perhaps, an optional matter that we should display a modicum of honesty in our dealings with each other, or that we should refrain from committing acts gross injustice against the weak in circumstances where they are not protected by the law. It might even be said that basic rules of this kind enshrine the collective wisdom of humanity, or at any rate of the particular society in which they are practised. But this very fact, if it is a fact, would diminish their importance for the persons I have in mind, who tend to think of the moral life as very much a personal affair, and to play down the framework of convention which constitutes public morality. Necessary as the latter is, it offers no scope for individual innovation or variety, and is in consequence scarcely to be counted as moral in any serious sense.

The difficulty with this is to know just what the field of morality is to cover once we exclude from it decent behaviour as conventionally practised. One suggestion, whose Kantian overtones are immediately obvious, is that it should strictly be confined to the inner life, morality being essentially a matter of the achievement of a pure heart, or if the term is preferred of personal integrity. The supreme moral virtue on this way of looking at the question would be sincerity; what would count would be not so much what one chose, but one's determination to stand by it once the choice was made. I should not want myself to dismiss this attitude as entirely worthless (it is plainly too widely shared to be discounted altogether); I confess, however, that I do not understand how anyone could take it to embody the whole truth about the subject. To argue in this way that sincerity is the highest, and indeed in the end the only, moral virtue is to open the door to moral nonsense of the most dangerous kind; it is to risk sacrificing the achievements of civilisation on the altar of romantic individualism, a procedure which is not made more rational by the thought that the sacrifice is being carried out in the name of civilisation itself. It seems to me to be a merit in Hegel, and a testimony to his grasp of moral reality, that he saw the limits of the fashionable morality of conscience, and refused to identify it with morality itself. As he argued (see especially *Philosophy of Right*, § 140), insistence on intention as the centre of morality can be used to justify conduct of any kind. But moralists should be interested in results as well as intentions; they should also observe that moral rules, just because they are rules, have interpersonal validity, and so cannot be a matter for exclusively personal choice. To that extent I regard the Hegelian comparison of moral with intellectual judgment as illuminating and correct.

Where Hegel is unsatisfying is that he apparently leaves no room for personal morality of any kind. He allows, of course, that moral agents shall have freely accepted the principles they apply, but has little or no interest in the cultivation of individual conscience for its own sake. Yet a man might argue that he feels obliged not just to fulfil his duties as a social being, but also to live up to certain standards in his personal life; he owes many things to his fellows, but he also owes something to himself. Or to put the point another way: a man needs not just to carry out his obligations, but to carry them out in a certain spirit; it is incumbent on him to be a good citizen or a good father or a good friend, but at least as important as any of these is the necessity of being a good man, that is, of cultivating his soul. It must be confessed that Hegel is insensitive to this whole dimension of the moral life; the exaggerations of its advocates among his contemporaries doubtless blinded him to its importance. It would be wrong, however, to think that he made the good life entirely a social affair. In the *Encyclopaedia* the section on 'Mind Objective', which corresponds in content to the *Philosophy of Right*, is followed by another on 'Absolute Mind', which treats of Art, Religion and Philosophy; the clear implication is that these topics fall outside the province of the state, and thus that there could well be what Bradley called an 'ideal' morality to complement the morality of 'my station and its duties' in which Hegel is primarily interested. Hegel might well have been unwilling to recognise explicitly that a man could justifiably put personal claims above the claims of the community, but he was certainly not unaware of the contention that there are wider loyalties than those we owe in our narrowly ethical capacity: loyalties we feel in so far as we practise the arts, engage in religious activities or seek the truth for its own sake. It would be quite false to suggest that Hegel was prepared to dismiss such loyalties as chimerical; he would undoubtedly have understood the dilemma of Gauguin, and even sympathised with its solution. No one before him, except perhaps Vico, had anything like the same grasp of the social function and the social connections of religion, yet he remained to the end a Lutheran Protestant in thinking that religion is at bottom a personal affair concerned with the salvation of an individual's soul. In short, he was not the totalitarian monster that some critics have seen in him. Nor, indeed, did he hold that in the sphere of morality proper prevailing codes must always be accepted without question; there was room for individual dissent even here, as in the well-known case of Socrates. Hegel's point was not that the right of free judgment in morals does not exist, but rather that it needs to be exercised at most on rare occasions. To make it central in morality, as so many of his contemporaries did, is to preclude the possibility of a working system of morals. As I have already pointed out, such a system depends on the acceptance of rules which are objective and hence interpersonal, and which accordingly cannot owe their validity to the fact that this or that moral agent has chosen to adhere to them.

IV. ETHICAL FORMALISM

We must next consider how Kant and Hegel compare as regards the *content* of their ethical systems. And here the first point to be stressed is that, on the surface at least, there are striking similarities between them. Both lay emphasis on the objective character of the moral law, which they take to be binding on agents without regard to their personal wishes; both argue that the content of the law is determined by rational principles and can accordingly be apprehended by reason. But this apparent agreement conceals substantial differences about the scope and nature of reason as the moral faculty.

According to Kant, the proper way to decide if a suggested course of action is morally legitimate is to ask yourself whether the maxim of the action could serve as a universal law. To engage in an act whose maxim cannot thus be universalised and at the same time to claim it as morally permissible is to fall into logical inconsistency, since from the moral point of view what holds for one man must hold for all others similarly circumstanced. The details of this doctrine are notoriously difficult, but we can perhaps elucidate it sufficiently for our present purposes on the following lines. By a 'maxim' Kant means, in his own words, 'the subjective principle of a volition':[21] an agent's maxim answers to the general description which can be given of the act when seen from the agent's point of view. Thus Kant gives as the maxim of the man who proposes to commit suicide: 'From self-love I make it my principle to shorten my life if its continuance threatens more evil than it promises pleasure';[22] the idea here is, I take it, that, if the man were to commit suicide, he could properly be described as shortening his life in circumstances where he believed its continuance promised more evil than pleasure for himself. And Kant's test of the moral acceptability of a maxim is whether or not it can be universalised without contradiction. In one group of cases, he tells us, we have only to think of the maxim as having general application to see that a contradiction is involved; in another we can indeed think of the maxim as having general application, but cannot consistently will that it should. A maxim which cannot govern the actions of all agents who find themselves in the same general circumstances, or which is such that the agent cannot consistently will it to have general application, is ruled out as incapable of serving as a moral law because incapable of the universality which is a formal characteristic of that law.

It is immediately obvious that the universalisation test, as thus interpreted, is purely negative: if applied successfully, it will show what ought not to be done, but will not tell us what we positively ought to do. When Hegel complains that Kant's standpoint involves 'no immanent doctrine of duties'[23] he may have had this point in mind. As he says:

If the definition of duty is taken to be the absence of contradiction, formal correspondence with itself – which is nothing but abstract indeterminacy stabilised – then no transition is possible to the specification of particular duties.[24]

But in fact Hegel advances a stronger thesis than this, that the test is not effective even when taken as purely negative. By itself it can rule out nothing, and hence 'by this means any wrong or immoral line of conduct may be justified'.[25]

How does Hegel get to this conclusion? As usual, his remarks are suggestive rather than specific, but it is possible to reconstruct his main line of thought without too much difficulty. Consider the following passage:

The absence of property contains in itself just as little contradiction as the non-existence of this or that nation, family, etc., or the death of the whole human race. But if it is already established on other grounds and presupposed that property and human life are to exist and be respected, then indeed it is a contradiction to commit theft or murder; a contradiction must be a contradiction of something, i.e. of some content presupposed from the start as a fixed principle. It is to a principle of that kind alone, therefore, that an action can be related either by way of correspondence or contradiction.[26]

To elucidate this it will be best to concentrate on Kant's own examples. Kant held that the maxim 'Whenever I believe myself short of money, I will borrow money and promise to pay it back, though I know this will never be done' could 'never rank as a universal law and be self-consistent, but must necessarily contradict itself'; if everyone were to act on this principle 'promising and the very purpose of promising'[27] would become impossible. We may agree that in these circumstances the whole institution of giving and accepting promises would collapse without possibility of revival. But it does not follow that a world without promises would be morally inferior to the existing world; all that Kant demonstrates is you cannot both accept the institution of promise-keeping and repudiate something which necessarily goes with it, namely that a person who makes a promise intends to carry it out. Hegel is quite correct in arguing that it is a presupposition of Kant's argument that it is right to keep promises: the very conclusion his appeal to the universalisation test is supposed to justify.

The effectiveness of Hegel's criticism comes out still more clearly if we turn to the other type of case Kant considers, that in which the universalisation of the maxim is conceivable but where Kant says that we nevertheless cannot will that it should hold as a universal law. Kant gives two examples to illustrate this, one concerned with cultivating one's talents, the other with helping other people in distress. I shall confine myself now to the second of these. Kant concedes that there might well be a world in which everybody kept to himself and did nothing to help those who needed help; he adds, however, that 'it is impossible to *will* that such a principle should hold everywhere as a universal law of nature. For a will which decided in this way would be at variance with itself'.[28] How exactly it would be is a notoriously difficult problem in Kantian exegesis, and here I can only suggest dogmatically that the best way to interpret the passage from Kant's point of view is to see him as supposing that the man who repudiates any obligation to help others might nevertheless in changed circumstances think that others *ought to* help him. His will would then be at variance with itself in that he would be (potentially) proclaiming a principle which he is at present actively disowning. But this would certainly not show that to refuse help to others in need is positively immoral. The man who both refuses and claims help is indeed involved in inconsistency, but he can get out of it in one of two ways: by recognising the obligation as it applies to himself, or by ceasing to maintain that others ought to observe it. In general, if you are in a position where you cannot consistently act on maxim m and make claim c, you can avoid the difficulty either by ceasing to act on maxim m or by giving up claim c. The weakness in Kant's argument is that he assumes that only one possibility is open to the agent, to give up acting on the maxim. And he took this step, as Hegel saw, because it seemed to him obvious from the first that human beings ought to help others in the circumstances described.

Hegel held, as we have already seen, that 'by this means', i.e. by appeal to the universalisation test, 'any wrong or immoral line of conduct may be justified'.[29] Talk of 'justification' is in point here only if we argue that a principle which passes the test automatically takes its place in a scheme of moral legislation, and we shall perhaps do well to consider here the weaker thesis that the test cannot rule any suggested moral principle out. That this thesis is in fact correct I shall now try to show by an example.

Under certain systems of totalitarian government children are encouraged to inform the police if they overhear their parents criticising the régime. Loyalty to the state, they are told, comes before loyalty to one's family, and even though the child's information may lead to the parents' punishment it is nevertheless right that it should be given. To the great majority of those living in other countries this practice of setting children against parents is morally abominable; it is one of the most revolting features of the whole totalitarian way of life. Kant himself, with his liberal outlook, would certainly have taken this view. But could a modern Kantian demonstrate to a convinced believer in totalitarianism the wrongness of this particular maxim of his? I very much doubt if he could.

Suppose first that he tried to argue that the maxim was such that we could not even conceive of its holding as a universal law, thus assimilating it to the case of false promises. What would it be like, we may imagine him asking, if not only were children to spy on parents, but further everyone who had special relations with others, as fellow-worker, member of the same social organisation or neighbour, for example, were to inform against them if he thought it proper. Mutual confidence would vanish altogether in such circumstances, and social life be quite impossible. Unfortunately for this argument as well as for humanity the world has witnessed, and is still witnessing, systems of government under which conditions are very much as here described. Mutual confidence in countries under such systems is doubtless very low, and life wellnigh impossible in the moral sense of the term. But it is not impossible in the physical sense, and so the argument fails to establish its point.

What then of the alternative of saying that, while such a system is certainly conceivable, no one could consistently will it to obtain? The contention would turn, no doubt, on the supposition that while we might all be complacent at the thought of spying on other people, or again at that of other people spying on each other, we should immediately grow indignant when we found ourselves being watched. There would be a contradiction between what we demanded for others and what we demanded for ourselves. But would such an attitude necessarily be found in a convinced totalitarian? Would not his view, if he were a genuine believer, be likely to be quite different? Persuaded as he is that the interests of the state come before those of any of its individual members, he will apply this principle to himself as much as to others, telling his children, for instance, that if ever they detect in him dangerous thoughts or counter-revolutionary tendencies they are to denounce him at once to the proper authorities, for to have such thoughts or tendencies is sabotage against the state and immoral in the highest degree. The behaviour of the accused in Koestler's novel *Darkness at Noon* is surely significant in this respect.

I do not wish these remarks to be taken as implying that I think that the universalisation test is entirely without value. In circumstances where an agent is firmly committed to a moral principle, it can bring home to him effectively the way in which he is disregarding the principle in his own case. But this, of course, confirms Hegel's point that appeal to the test presupposes that some types of conduct are accepted as right: except on this basis it can demonstrate nothing. It is interesting in this connection to observe that Kantian commentators have suggested that there may have been intuitionist elements in Kant's ethical thought (cf. Paton: *The Categorical Imperative*, p. 138), though how he could have consistently supported ethical intuitionism in view of his general attitude to the possibility of intellectual intuition is not apparent. Be that as it may, the fact remains that Kant did believe that certain moral conclusions 'leap to the eye'.[30] The criticism which Hegel brings against him has thus every appearance of being well founded.

What is less clear is how Hegel himself can insist on the charge, in view of his own commitment to rationalism in ethics. That logical considerations alone can decide nothing about the desirability of this or that form of conduct is a thesis we might expect to see advanced by a Hume, but scarcely by a Hegel. The passage quoted from Hegel on p. 22 recalls in its very wording Hume's famous declaration that "tis not contrary to reason to prefer the destruction of the whole world to the scratching of my finger'.[31] Yet there is no evidence whatsoever to suggest that Hegel had any sympathy with Hume's position in ethics, which struck him as a combination of subjectivism and scepticism. Hume's doctrine that 'moral distinctions [are] not derived from reason',[32] with its complement that they are to be connected with a moral sense, is not even mentioned in the brief summary Hegel gives of Hume on ethics in his lectures on the history of philosophy. There is every indication that he thought it so far from the truth as not to be worth discussing.

To understand how Hegel could thus reject Kant's form of ethical objectivism without regarding himself as committed to a theory like Hume's we need to examine his moral psychology, which clearly differed at important points from that of both his distinguished predecessors. It would, however, be premature to undertake the examination at this stage, and I shall proceed instead to consider some further criticisms Hegel makes of Kant, not this time of his ethical theory under that name, but in the guise of a critique of what Hegel calls 'the moral point of view', *die moralische Weltanschauung*. These criticisms are made in his first major work the *Phenomenology*, but that Hegel had no wish to retract them is shown by his referring to them explicitly in the paragraph of the *Philosophy of Right* on which this section has been a comment (§ 135).

V. THE CONTRADICTIONS OF
KANTIAN MORALITY

'The moral point of view', like the other positions explored in the *Phenomenology*, is an attitude to life rather than a formal philosophy. Hegel's own interest in it is twofold: he sees it both as a stage in human history and as a partial anticipation of the wholly adequate standpoint of which he claims himself to be master. Regarded as a stage in human history 'the moral point of view' is alleged to offer a synthesis of the ethical world of the Greeks, where spirit was sunk in objectivity, and of the individualist culture of post-Hellenic times, when spirit was 'self-estranged'; it claims, that is to say, to combine the element of universal law which is essential to morality with the element of individual choice which is also essential. Regarded as a partial anticipation of Hegel's own position it is to be seen as a form of idealism, and deserves this title because of the emphasis it puts on the autonomy of the will and hence on mind. It is, however, an incomplete form of idealism, since it presents mind as active in an essentially alien world, and can offer no intelligible account of how its activity is possible.

Hegel works out this charge by arguing that there are two main points at which the position he is examining is unstable. The first concerns the relationship between the moral agent and external reality. The moralist (it will be obvious from the sequel that Hegel has the Kantian moralist in mind throughout) makes the sharpest of distinctions between himself as a pure moral being and nature as the setting in which he acts. Nature is governed by one set of laws, the moral agent by quite another. Nature has no concern with moral consciousness, the moral consciousness no concern with nature, in so far as nothing really matters to it except its own inner purity. But the fact remains that the moral agent has to act, which means that he must carry out purposes in the world, with

the result that he cannot dissociate himself from the world altogether but must in some measure at least subordinate it to himself.
The possibility of successful action rests on something more than
inner purity of heart or the right direction of the will, as Kant
recognised when he made the existence of God a postulate of pure
practical reason. Belief in God, as he explains, is irrelevant to the
acceptance of duties, but vitally involved in the attempt to carry
them out, since the agent needs assurance that his most carefully
considered and morally pure intentions will not be thwarted by an
alien nature. Or to put the matter more crudely, as Kant himself
was apt to do, he needs to feel confident that his efforts to realise
the good are likely to result in a state of affairs which is satisfactory
to himself and others. He gets that confidence by postulating a
God who proportions happiness to virtue, and so moralises
nature in the required way.

Before considering Hegel's criticisms of these views we must
turn to the second respect in which he believes the moral point of
view to be unstable. This concerns the make-up of the moral
agent himself. We have spoken so far as if nature existed outside
man as a setting in which he has to act, but the fact is, of course,
that it exists within him as well. To quote Hegel's own description
of the situation:

Nature is not merely this completely free external mode in which,
as a bare pure object, consciousness has to realise its purpose. Consciousness is *per se* essentially something *for* which this other detached
reality exists, i.e. it is *itself* something contingent and natural. This
nature, which is properly its own, is *sensibility*, which, taking the form
of volition, in the shape of impulses and inclinations, has by itself a
determinate essential being of its own, i.e. has specific single purposes,
and thus is opposed to pure will with its pure purpose. In contrast with
this opposition, however, pure consciousness rather takes the relation
of sensibility to it, the absolute unity of sensibility with it, to be the
essential fact. Both of these, pure thought and sensibility, are essentially and inherently *one* consciousness.[33]

The fact that the moral agent has natural impulses means that he
is confronted by a double problem: he has to moralise the world,
in the way already described, and he has to dominate or domesti-
cate the sensuous elements within himself. But the second part of

the task is on the face of it more difficult than the first. Given moral belief in God's existence on the Kantian model the moral agent need never be, to use a phrase of Kant's own, 'circumscribed in his endeavour':[34] he can go ahead with his plans in the confidence that no unkind fate will thwart their execution. This is because the postulate of God's existence serves to cancel the alien character of the natural world. But there can be no question of simply abolishing the sensuous part of human nature in a similar way, since moral consciousness itself exists as a counter to sensibility. Remove the natural inclinations, and the moral will loses its *raison d'être*, which is to fight against and overcome the passions. We therefore find it laid down in the moral view of the world that harmony between morality and sensibility is something which can never be fully achieved, but at best approached asymptotically. As Kant himself expressed it, we need to postulate 'an infinitely enduring existence',[35] in the course of which the moral agent is engaged in an endless progress towards moral perfection. We need, in other words, to accept the immortality of the soul as an article of moral belief.

Hegel shows in these passages that the doctrine of the postulates of practical reason, so far from being a curious excrescence on the Kantian system, is rather of its essence; to dispense with them would be to rob the whole structure of all its plausibility. But this is not to say that he is prepared to accept the postulates. On the contrary, he regards them as at best a makeshift, designed to disguise glaring contradictions. The moral view of the world is at bottom radically incoherent, and the postulates only distract attention from that fact. For it remains true first that morality is at once indifferent to and intimately concerned with nature: it aspires to ignore it and withdraw wholly into itself, but knows very well that it cannot do so just because of the obligation to act. Secondly, it has to be allowed that morality is committed both to the destruction of the natural passions and to their preservation: to the former because, in any conflict between reason and the inclinations, it is axiomatic that reason ought to triumph, to the latter because moral reason needs the natural passions both as its antithesis and its instrument. As Hegel puts it, 'morality is only moral consciousness qua negative force'.[36] It follows, he argues, that the man who adopts 'the moral point of view' is not really in earnest with morality: despite his professions, he does not want to see the total domestication of his sensuous nature, and that this is so is shown in his acceptance of the second postulate, which puts off the completion of the process to a future which is infinitely distant. He is happy only in occupying the middle ground in which morality is seen as an endless struggle, though one in which progress towards victory is always supposed to be possible. Yet how, Hegel asks, can we assume even this much? If the struggle between flesh and spirit is to be seen as unending, there can be no question of an advance to better things, the more so because, in these terms, 'advancing in morality would really mean approaching its disappearance'.[37] Nor on this view can we hold to the description of the situation assumed in the first postulate, according to which God is needed to proportion happiness to virtue. Vice and virtue will not be identifiable in these conditions; to speak of someone as immoral will be an act of pure caprice, and the judgment that the wicked flourish in this world will be 'an expression of envy, which covers itself up in the cloak of morality'.[38] In short, moral activity as here conceived is a fraud, and the moral man at best confused, at worst a conscious hypocrite.

In the foregoing paragraphs I have attempted to set down the main points of a complicated argument, but I must warn the reader that the version I offer is both simplified and tidied up in comparison with the original. Hegel lays particular emphasis on the 'dissimulation' involved in the moral point of view, a feature which comes out in the way those who hold that position shift continually from one pole of their contradictory standpoint to the other; I have said nothing about this. Nor have I been able to make any reference to a third aspect of the Kantian doctrine which Hegel considers in this connection, the representation of duties as divine commands which is developed in *Religion within the Bounds of Mere Reason*. Hegel's presentation of this point seems to me both arbitrary and singularly difficult to connect with any live issue in current philosophy. But it must be admitted that his whole manner and style of argument in the *Phenomenology* are about as different as they could be from the sober procedures of present-day analytic philosophers. Instead of a straightforward case developed logically from point to point we find ourselves confronted with a series of sketches, some of them suggestive, others seemingly arbitrary, and all of them couched in language which looks precise but is bafflingly opaque when examined from close to. The comment is at times pointed and penetrating, but equally seems in places wholly forced; the presentation of views to be examined is clearly not wholly caricature, yet too often appears to be determined by nothing so much as the need to fit into a place in Hegel's peculiar system. The whole plan of the *Phenomenology*, which explores positions that have been historically held but does it without historical documentation, facilitates this procedure: if anyone objects that he is being unfair to Kant, Hegel can always reply that he is dealing not with Kant but with a type of position like Kant's. The question then arises whether the refutations he produces are of views which are genuinely held rather than artificially set up. It is part of a general difficulty of knowing what to make of Hegel's strange arguments and just how seriously to take them.

What can we in fact make of the criticisms of 'the moral point of view'? One thing at least is clear, and that is the lessons Hegel wants to draw for a sound ethics. Such an ethics must not, in the first place, be an ethics of mere integrity; it must not make the sharp Kantian distinction between the moral agent and the world in which he lives. Morality, despite Kant's initial suggestions, involves performance as well as intention, and ethics must recognise this fact and explain how it is possible. Secondly, a satisfactory moral philosophy must give an altogether different account from that found in Kant of the relationship of moral reason and the inclinations. The Kantian doctrine which makes practical reason in effect the godlike element in man and writes down the passions as belonging to his animal nature amounts to a form of dualism as objectionable as any to be found in Descartes. The unity of the human being is entirely lost on this account, whose internal mechanics are in any case dubious, since the elements it identifies at once claim to be independent and have their existence in relation one to another. A man can no more be a bare compound of pure moral will and animal passions than he can be a bare compound of pure Cartesian intellect and bodily senses. In urging this point Hegel was adopting a position with which modern philosophers can readily sympathise.

How exactly Hegel thought he could do justice to these points in his own ethical theory is a subject I shall be taking up shortly. Meantime, however, it is important to stress that to see sense in the criticisms of Kant just outlined is not to endorse everything Hegel says in comment on 'the moral point of view'. The surprising doctrine that the moral man cannot be in earnest with morality can certainly not be accepted as it stands. Hegel argues that, on Kant's premises, perfecting of the moral will would entail the disappearance of morality, since there would then be nothing for the moral agent to struggle against, and draws the conclusion that the Kantian moralist cannot really want what he says he wants. The argument has a certain empirical shrewdness, for it is true that those who fight against evils do not always welcome their complete disappearance: witness Graham Greene's story of the nuns in Africa who had spent their lives in combating a particular disease and had mixed feelings when the disease was eradicated by modern medicine. But it is scarcely cogent from the theoretical point of view. Hegel forgets, in the first place, that Kant puts forward the notion of a holy will as one which is evidently better than ours: a being possessed of such a will would act as it should without feeling under obligation to do so and without having any counter-inclination. And though Kant nowhere suggests that human beings can attain to this condition, he is not committed to the view that those who form good habits and are for this reason less troubled by temptation are inferior to those whose every moral decision is reached after an internal struggle. Will is manifested in the fostering and maintaining of virtuous dispositions just as it is in the man whose better and worse selves are in continual conflict.

What is correct in Hegel's contention is that the moralist wants not just a particular result, but a particular result attained in a

33

particular way: he is undoubtedly in earnest in demanding the triumph of good over evil, but he wants to see it brought about through moral effort. If men behaved as they should through sheer uncultivated good nature, or if (to take a possibility Kant considers) they acted as they ought only because they saw clearly that it would be to their advantage in the long run, something valuable would be lost from the world. The moralist, being faced with a situation in which, often at any rate, duty pulls in one direction and inclination in another, not unnaturally puts stress on good will, a concept which would have no application in the conditions just mentioned. But it does not follow from this that he is interested in good will *and nothing else*, despite the apparent implications of Kant's remarks at the beginning of the *Grundlegung*. The presence of good will may be a necessary condition for the attaining of a morally satisfactory result; it is certainly not a sufficient condition.

When Hegel accuses the moralist of fraud and hypocrisy he makes a plausible case only by comparing unlikes – the situation we are actually in, and the situation we should be in if everyone acted automatically as he ought. He says, in effect, that the moral agent does not want to bring about the latter situation. This is true, but it remains to be noticed first that there is no question of his bringing it about (he must take men as they are), and secondly, that his indifference or even hostility to this goal does not mean that he is indifferent to the attaining of concrete moral results. To say that he is is like saying that a mathematician cannot really want to solve a problem because the only solution which will satisfy him is one produced through intellectual effort. An omniscient being would be innocent of intellectual difficulties and therefore of intellectual triumphs, but this fact has no bearing at all on the question whether human thinkers really want to solve the problems they seemingly set themselves.

VI. VALUE, FACT AND THE MORALITY OF LOVE

I turn now at length to Hegel's positive views, and shall lead into them by considering some curious remarks he makes about 'ought' and 'is'. This sounds a fashionable subject, but in fact Hegel's treatment of it is poles apart from that of the contemporary analytic philosopher. The latter is interested in the *logical* question how, if at all, statements setting out what is the case can lend support to judgments about what ought to be; in insisting on the dichotomy of fact and value, as he often does, he is wanting to point out the very different roles which are played in discourse by the two kinds of utterance. But when Hegel discusses 'ought' and 'is' the problem which is uppermost in his mind is that of what authority can be claimed for the judgment that something ought to be if we sharply separate 'fact' from 'value'; he questions the legitimacy of the separation not on grounds of logic, but on the ground that it is *morally* intolerable. No doubt his conclusions, if correct, have implications which bear on the logical problem with which modern philosophers are occupied, but he is not himself concerned with that problem in any direct way.

Hegel's views about 'ought' and 'is' are perhaps best approached through his early essay 'The Spirit of Christianity and its Fate'. This essay dates from the period when Hegel was trying to work his philosophy out, and the opinions it expresses differ in a number of important ways from those found in his main works (like his other *Jugendschriften*, it was not published by Hegel himself). On the point with which we are concerned now, however, it is instructive. Hegel offers in the essay a sort of philosophical history of the moral and religious life of the Jews, which begins with Abraham, continues through Moses and culminates in the moral teaching of Jesus. Ancient Jewish life as Hegel saw it was not an attractive affair, since the Jews were a passive and spiritless people who had enslaved themselves to their tyrannical God in return for material help. Everything they did was regulated by commandments, and these commandments had simply to be accepted by the Jewish people; it was not possible for individuals to question them, any more than a private soldier can question military orders. The right of individual judgment, so far as it existed among the Jews, was introduced by Jesus who, as Hegel saw him, professed to 'fulfil' the ancient law, but in fact transformed its character. Instead of subjecting them to a series of objective commands, expressed in the form 'Thou shalt . . .', Jesus sought to awaken in men's hearts the desire to behave in a better way, by appealing to the notion of love. The Mosaic code had demanded that men engage in or refrain from certain actions without reference to their personal judgment; Jesus bade them love one another, and thus proposed to substitute disinterested inclination for respect for duty as the main moral motive. For various reasons which are now irrelevant his main effort failed, but it nevertheless struck Hegel as constituting a profound moral advance. And to underline its bearing on the conditions of his own time Hegel went out of his way to draw a comparison between the situation of the Jews under the Mosaic arrangements and that of the moral subject as depicted in the Kantian philosophy. Just as there was total opposition between Jehovah and his creatures, with no option for the latter but to obey, so there was total opposition in Kant's system between 'pure' reason and the 'empirical' inclinations, which were coerced rather than persuaded into acquiescing in reason's commands. In Hegel's view the gulf revealed here had to be bridged, and could be if Kant's type of view were abandoned in favour of a morality of love.

The terms in which Hegel tries to work this argument out reveal his preoccupation, even at this early date, with philosophical issues of the widest kind. Kant's legalistic approach to morality was not an isolated phenomenon: it was part of a general attempt, natural but nevertheless radically misconceived, to comprehend what was living and therefore individual in abstract formulae, to capture life in conceptual terms. The primary mistake in the whole notion of a categorical imperative issuing from moral reason was its abstract character: being the product of thought it could represent only one side of human nature. As Hegel put it in a relatively lucid passage in which he contrasts the morality of the Old Testament with that of the Sermon on the Mount:

A command can express no more than an ought or a shall, because it is a universal, but it does not express an 'is'; and this at once makes plain its deficiency. Against such commands Jesus sets virtue, i.e. a loving disposition, which makes the content of the command super-fluous and destroys its form as a command, because that form implies an opposition between a commander and something resisting the command.[39]

The 'righteousness' professed by the 'sons of duty'[40] involves a split between the universal (the general rule) which is 'master' and the particular inclinations which are 'mastered'. 'Virtue', by contrast, constitutes 'a righteousness of a new kind',[41] marked not by legalism, standing upon rights and a prim consciousness of rectitude, but by what amounts to open-hearted sympathy. In it

the moral disposition, etc., ceases to be universal, opposed to inclina-tion, and inclination ceases to be particular, opposed to the law, and therefore this correspondence of law and inclination is life and, as the relation of differents to one another, love; i.e. it is an 'is'.[42]

We must not be misled in this connection by the form of pro-nouncement used by exponents of the new morality. No doubt Jesus spoke in the imperative mood, but

this turn of phrase is a command in a sense quite different from that of the 'shalt' of the moral imperative. It is only the sequel to the fact that, when life is conceived in thought or given expression, it acquires a *form* alien to it, a conceptual form, while, on the other hand, the moral imperative is, as a universal, in *essence* a concept.[43]

These passages clearly express a violent revulsion on Hegel's part against accepted moral attitudes, indeed in places against morality itself (the 'spirit of Jesus', we are told, was a spirit 'raised above morality').[44] Like many others of his time and age, the young Hegel found the moral set-up of the society in which he lived both rigid and alien. The rules it imposed were too abstractly general to fit particular cases, and there was a sugges-tion, which Hegel saw as obviously immoral, that once they were complied with any other conduct was permissible. Worse than this, however, was the fact that they in no sense sprang from the hearts of the persons to whom they applied; they represented the voice of a foreign authority. It may seem odd that this complaint should be brought against Kant, after the stress he had laid on the need for moral agents to will the law rather than merely take it as given. But, as we have seen, Hegel argued that the voice of reason in Kant was as remote from the living being as was Jehovah from the ancient Jews. The pretence that I give my assent to the moral law because my reason accepts it has no justification, for reason is not by any means the whole person. The terms in which Kant described the moral situation – in particular the use of phrases like 'law', 'command' and 'obligation' – showed that, despite everything, his conception of it was authoritarian. But instead of locating moral authority in God or some external body, Kant located it in an abstraction within ourselves.

In demanding that the ethical gap between 'ought' and 'is' be bridged Hegel was asking for an account of morality which would show it to be internal rather than foreign to the persons it embraced, and this was a requirement which he continued to make long after he had discarded the solution put forward in this early work. That solution clearly owed something to Aristotle and perhaps even to Hume; if we asked if it was, broadly, on rationalist or anti-rationalist lines, we should have to say the latter. In this respect as well as in its cavalier attitude to the established order it scarcely fits the conventional picture of Hegel. But there is another way in which its doctrines do point forward to his later philosophy.

When Hegel found the 'modification of life'[45] which was to overcome the opposition between reason and inclination in 'love', his choice of the latter term was undoubtedly connected with its use in the Christian gospels. The Christian community was to be animated by the spirit of love, and this was to be possible because its members were to see each other in a new light: not as isolated individuals each pursuing his private purposes, but as members of a wider whole, concerned with a corporate aim. In embracing Christianity men 'died to themselves' in order to 'find themselves'; henceforth their reality was to be part of the body of Christ. It would, of course, be entirely false to suggest that Hegel was unaware of the special circumstances in which these claims could be plausibly made. He knew very well that the early Christians formed a small and restricted group, and he gave particular attention to the question how that group with its free internal life was transformed into the very different organisation, dominated by 'positive' elements, which the Christian Church presently became. He was also aware of, and went out of his way to stress, the very complex nature of modern society. From a certain point of view it was perfectly correct to see in that society nothing but a set of atomic individuals each seeking his personal satisfaction. But this was not the whole truth on the subject, for in so far as he belonged to the state as opposed to civil society man was, even in modern conditions, part of a wider whole. If he were no longer engaged on a crusade, he was in an important sense constituted by his social relations and thus bound up with his fellow-citizens. And the possibility of finding a satisfactory rationale for ethics depended on that fact.

I shall be trying to explain this position further in the next section. Meantime, I want to suggest that though the ethical doctrine sketched in this early essay is obviously incomplete, the views it puts forward have a certain importance both from the negative and from the positive point of view. The criticisms of Kant are unfamiliar, but not therefore negligible; the notion of a morality of love leaves many questions unanswered, but at least indicates possible lines on which to solve a problem which has worried practical men more than moral philosophers. What is remarkable about the whole discussion is, indeed, the freedom with which Hegel challenges accepted views and probes into problems which they leave unresolved. If only he could have matched the vigour of his thought with skill in self-expression, he might well have transformed the course of subsequent discussion on this whole subject.

VII. VALUE, FACT AND CONCRETE ETHICS

In 'The Spirit of Christianity' the shortcomings of morality are to be overcome through membership of the Christian community, in which individuals lose their particularity and yet gain an enhanced sense of purpose. In Hegel's mature philosophy the same general view is taken, but the role of the church is now filled by the state or, as Hegel sometimes expresses it, 'the nation' (*das Volk*). It is the nation or the state which constitutes the ultimate unity which must be presupposed if the actions of individual men and women, including their moral actions, are to be made intelligible. For men are, fundamentally, social beings, and the nation or the state is the true social whole.

It must be made clear from the first that this doctrine does not involve the impossible consequence that individual persons do not exist as such, or possess at best an inferior form of existence. Individuals exist for Hegel exactly as they do for the rest of us; they are, indeed, the only concrete existents in the mental sphere. But their status is not what it is commonly taken to be: contrary to popular thought on the subject, they are not self-contained atoms each complete in himself. To explain how a human being feels, thinks or behaves you need to take account of something more than the human being himself; you need the notion of a continuing society of such beings, each of whom participates in a common life. If there were no individual persons, there could be no such society. But equally if there were no society individual persons as we know them would be unthinkable, since it is from society that they derive their most fundamental ways of thinking and acting.

The reader may be willing to grant that many important human activities are social in character, while still remaining suspicious of Hegel's exploitation of this very obvious truth. For after all it is one thing to claim that much if not all of our thinking and doing requires a social context, and so presupposes a wider continuing whole, and another to identify this whole with the state. Are there not social unities of many kinds, some narrower than the state or nation, others altogether wider? What an individual does in his capacity as a son or a father presupposes the family unit and the social organisation which goes with that, which is something short of the state. What he does as a workman or an employer presupposes economic arrangements of varying complexity; in some cases the network of relationships involved is of limited and local extent, in others it is coextensive with the nation, in yet others it transcends national boundaries. As a soldier or a civil servant a man operates within the context of the state, and it is to that institution that we must refer if we are to make sense of his activities. But is it clear that the same reference must be made if our concern is with his religious life or with the career he pursues as a scientist or a musician? And if it is not, by what right do we connect moral life in the concrete with the state? Could not the moral agent claim, and does he not claim, that he owes allegiance not just to his fellow-citizens, but to the whole of humanity?

It would be quite wrong to suppose that these questions had not occurred to Hegel, and indeed we have already had occasion to glance at some of his answers. I shall now sketch his position in rather more detail, and try in doing so to indicate why he lays particular emphasis on the state.

The most primitive form of concrete ethical life, according to Hegel, is that of the family. Here we have to do with a unity which is so close-knit that the question of individual rights comes up only as it begins to dissolve; up to that point each of the members of the family constitutes no more than a 'specific moment within the whole'.[46] The family has a natural basis in physical love between the sexes, but it is for all that a moral institution since marriage is deliberately entered into. 'Marriage, and especially monogamy, is one of the absolute principles on which the ethical life of a community depends.'[47] The partners to a marriage freely consent to merge their separate individualities in a new whole which will henceforth embrace both; from the narrowly personal point of view they seem to be restricting themselves by re-nouncing particular liberties, but in fact their union is 'their liberation, since in it they attain their substantive self-conscious-ness'.[48] Hegel presumably does not mean that a bachelor or a spinster cannot lead a satisfactory self-conscious life; his point is rather that marriage multiplies the opportunities for satisfaction by opening up possibilities of common action which are not available to single persons. The unmarried can certainly have children, but they cannot (or could not in Hegel's day) bring them up in the bosom of the family and thus enjoy the full de-lights of parenthood. Nor again can they participate in ownership of the family property, the permanent stock of possessions which belongs to no member in particular but is common to all of them. What Hegel calls 'labour and care for a common possession'[49] is, as he insists, fundamentally different from personal enrichment; it may involve mere greed, but something else is present too, namely the sense of a good which extends beyond the individual. Similarly sexual life in marriage can involve physical lust, but has an ethical side as well in so far as it connects with and symbolises other aspects of the union.

Many of Hegel's detailed remarks about the family now seem outmoded, but this is of minor importance when set beside his firm grasp of the principle that the family is a moral institution whose demands are not seen by those involved as imposed from without. It must not be thought, however, that he recommends the family as a model to be followed. For one thing, he sees that it is, as an institution, inherently unstable, since it dies away and has to be reconstituted afresh as each generation grows up. More importantly, however, he criticises it for allowing too little sub-jective freedom to its individual members. In the family situation the good of the family as a whole takes precedence over all other considerations, and this is a state of affairs which modern man will not tolerate. Hence the introduction of legislation which permits a man to dispose of his property to persons outside the family circle, and hence the dissolution of family life in 'civil society', the sphere in which individuals pursue satisfactions which are essentially private.

What Hegel has to say about civil or bourgeois society is based on his reading of contemporary political economists, whose importance he was quick to appreciate. He saw as they did that men living in towns had developed without any preliminary planning an elaborate system for the satisfaction of their wants and needs, a system which had profound effects on the structure of their lives and might well have profound effects on society as a whole. But whereas the economists saw their task as being that of 'explaining mass-relationships and mass-movements in their complexity and their qualitative and quantitative character',[50] by revealing the simple principles which underlay them, Hegel was interested in the wider bearings of the whole phenomenon, and in particular in demonstrating that the system of civil society was not and could not be self-contained.

He used two main arguments in support of this conclusion. First, he pointed out that bourgeois economic life can be a going concern only if it is complemented by institutions which operate on a different principle from that of private profit. This applies most obviously to the whole apparatus of law and law-enforcement which is increasingly called for as economic organisation grows in complexity; it applies again to the public services, water, drainage and so on, which are required if life in towns is to proceed smoothly, to the need for police services and for provision for the impoverished who, now that they have become 'sons of civil society',[51] can no longer look to their families for support. Paradoxically, the effect of letting individuals have freedom to maximise their private profit is to increase the need for a firm public authority.

Secondly, Hegel argued that, considered simply as an economic system, bourgeois society contains the seeds of its own destruction, and here he anticipated all the main points in Marx's criticism. The pursuit of profit leads to a vast increase not only in population and industry but also in specialisation of economic function, and this in turn results in the appearance on the scene of a class tied to a limited kind of work and therefore unable 'to feel and enjoy the broader freedoms and especially the intellectual benefits of civil society'.[52] With the concentration of wealth in fewer and fewer hands and the consequent depression of the living standards of these workers there is created a 'rabble of paupers',[53] deprived of self-respect because deprived of the opportunity to maintain themselves through their own work and efforts. And this introduces a problem which bourgeois society cannot solve, at least on its own ground, for to subsidise this rabble without calling on them to work is to violate the individualist principle of this whole society, while to give them the opportunity to work is to encourage overproduction in conditions where there is no chance of a corresponding increase in the consumers' market. 'It hence becomes apparent that despite an excess of wealth civil society is not rich enough, i.e. its own resources are insufficient to check excessive poverty and the creation of a penurious rabble.'[54] The only remedy available to a civil society in this condition is 'to push beyond its own limits and seek markets, and so its necessary means of subsistence, in other lands which are either deficient in the goods it has overproduced, or else generally backward in industry, etc.'.[55] A 'mature'[56] civil society is thus driven by its own 'inner dialectic'[57] to colonisation, and this is something again which calls for direction by public authority.

Hegel's answer to the criticisms made on p. 41, so far as they concern the family and economic life, is thus that both presuppose the state. Family life cannot withstand the pressures of the modern world, and gives way to the individualistic organisation of civil society, which in turn points forward to public authority exercised in the name of the nation. It might be said in comment on this that capitalism by Hegel's own confession is international, and has grown increasingly so since the time of his death. I suspect, however, that Hegel would resist the suggestion that international finance and business can operate in entire freedom from national political control, and simply deny the Marxist thesis that the state is a creature of the dominant economic class. The experience of the post-war world might be adduced in support of the first of these points: the involvement of the state in economic affairs is now such that it is difficult to claim that there still exists any such thing as a non-political economic structure. As for the second, direct proof or disproof of Hegel's contention is hard to come by, but we can at least appeal in his support to the strong evidence of national feeling and aspirations as seen in modern politics. That this could all be artificially fostered to suit the purposes of the ruling class is certainly thinkable, but it is not very likely all the same.

This brings us to the state, which Hegel describes in the following terms:

The state is the actuality of the ethical Idea. It is ethical mind *qua* the substantial will manifest and revealed to itself, knowing and thinking itself, accomplishing what it knows and in so far as it knows it. The state exists immediately in custom, mediately in individual self-consciousness, knowledge, and activity, while self-consciousness in virtue of its sentiment towards the state finds in the state, as its essence and the end and product of its activity, its substantive freedom.[58]

'This substantial unity', Hegel adds,

is an absolute unmoved end in itself, in which freedom comes into its supreme right. On the other hand this final end has supreme right against the individual, whose supreme duty it is to be a member of the state.[59]

The first requisite in understanding these apparently provocative pronouncements is to grasp that Hegel did not take the state to be a merely political structure, or a structure which is partly political and partly legal. The merely political state (the 'external state', as Hegel calls it) exists even in civil society, but it is not this poor abstraction which Hegel identifies with 'the actuality of the ethical Idea'. A better conception of what he was after can be got if we speak not of the state but of the nation. The activities of the state as Hegel conceives it cover every aspect of national life, and are thus cultural as much as political, educational as much as economic. The state is the manifestation of the spirit of the nation, which is continuously active in a wide variety of spheres.

What then is the relationship between a state and its individual members? We can perhaps clarify Hegel's position on this point if we return for a moment to his account of the family. In entering on the marriage relationship the partners ostensibly restrict themselves, but in fact acquire opportunities for wider self-development. When the marriage is established they will not see the restraints it involves as imposed upon them, but accept them as a necessary condition of the richer life they have obtained. Similarly the demands of the state seem at first constricting for the individual, but their true effect is to liberate him by extending the possibilities of purposive action for him. The duties and restraints which go with membership of a nation should hence not be seen as evils which a rational man would avoid if he could, but as means to an altogether better life. To take them in the former way, common as it is, is to be involved in a fundamental misunderstanding of the relationship between the individual and the state. Just as the family was not something alien to its members but the wider whole in which those members had their being, so the state is not a foreign framework in which the unhappy individual finds himself compelled to live, but rather something continuous with himself. The state, as Hegel puts it, is mind made objective; it is, roughly, a set of institutions, activities and ways of going on which are the product of many minds and on which individual minds are unceasingly dependent. An individual constantly draws in his thinking on ideas and methods which are the common possession of his community; he makes them his own, perhaps modifies them in minor details and hands them on to others in his turn. If you ask whether they are his own ideas or someone else's, he finds it hard to say. But the antithesis, though useful in particular contexts, is nevertheless in general misleading, since 'mine' and 'yours' are unimportant in this area of essentially collective achievement.

It should now be possible to appreciate why Hegel thought that reference to the state would solve the basic problems of ethics. Each of us regards himself as intimately bound up with his country, a fact which comes out most plainly in times of war and national danger, but which is also evidenced both in the simple man's pride in her achievements and the liberal intellectual's shame at her misdeeds. The relationship between a man and his country is less intimate than that between a man and his family, but the two run parallel in so far as neither involves absolute opposition between terms which are wholly distinct. The fortunes of my country are in some sense my fortunes, just as the fortunes of my family are. It follows that the voice in which my country addresses me, if there is any question of this, will not be a foreign voice. Or to put the matter more plainly, the restraints my country lays upon me and the duties it requires of me will not be imposed from without; they will not have the alien character which Hegel complains of as present in Kant's ethical system. In submitting to them I shall not be submitting myself to external control, but obeying what is really an extension of myself. In these circumstances the demand Kant made that the moral subject be autonomous, but which he was himself unable to satisfy because of his abstract conception of moral reason, will finally be met. The moral law, instead of being the pronouncement of pure but therefore inhuman reason, will be shown to be involved in our most ordinary activities, and will be accepted as reasonable just because of that fact.

There is another way in which Hegel thinks that reference to the state overcomes the deficiencies of the Kantian outlook. As we saw, one point in that outlook which he could not accept was the gulf it left between fact and value. The morally valuable was an everlasting ought to be, while the facts were eternally unmoralised. In Hegel's concrete ethics the gap is supposed to be bridged thanks to the fact that morality is embodied in institutions and actual practices, or is intimately bound up with these. The man who wonders what obligation he has to pay his debts, for instance, need no longer be told an unconvincing story about the categorical imperative requiring him to do so, but can be shown instead the way in which the honouring of such obligations is a condition of the whole complex system of credit, without which advanced economic life would be impossible. The rule which is brought forward in a case of this sort gains in authority from the simple fact that it is widely observed; its force is enhanced again by its connecting with a wide range of human wants and purposes. And if it is said that these advantages are purchased at the price of heteronomy in the Kantian sense, Hegel will reply that he does not recognise the Kantian dichotomy between reason and the inclinations, but nevertheless provides for the autonomy of the moral agent in his own way.

The main points of strength in Hegel's position seem to be these. First, that human activities, though by no means all of a communal nature, normally presuppose a community setting. Second, that men are apt to look on the community they belong to, above all if it is a modern nation state, as being their own in a special sense, with the result that they feel involved in its acts and even answerable for them. Third, that the observation of moral rules and restraints is bound up with the smooth functioning of a community; unless such rules and restraints are widely accepted in the society few if any distinctively human activities will be possible. Fourth, that pressure to observe moral rules of the type in question is predominantly social pressure, and owes its effectiveness in large part to the force of example. We do as we ought, in these matters, because other people in our community are doing as they ought. The fact that these others are persons we know, or at least recognise as belonging to the same group as ourselves, is all-important in this connection.

VIII. CRITIQUE OF CONCRETE ETHICS

I come now to some criticisms. One which will have occurred to
many readers is that Hegel exaggerates the organic nature of the
state, or again lays undue emphasis on the extent to which individuals feel themselves to be bound up with their community.
It may be useful in this connection to distinguish between positive
and negative adherence to a community. We are all involved in
national activities in the negative sense that we could not do the
things we do unless the state were in a certain way viable; we
could not, for example, do business or educate our children
unless there were relatively stable political conditions, an effective
legal system and so on. Since we obviously want to do things of
the sort mentioned, we must be willing to accept whatever makes
them possible, which means accepting the state with all the
obligations that it involves. But though we tolerate the imposi-
tions of the state, legal and moral, in this passive way, it does not
follow that we actively welcome them, still less that we look on
the state as an extension of ourselves. We might do that if we
were living in a time of national resurgence or national peril, but
not otherwise. Hegel shows where he stands on this subject
nowhere more clearly than in his celebrated pronouncements
about the ethical significance of war. In the *Philosophy of Right*[60]
he quotes from an early essay of his in which he had said that by
the agency of war

the ethical health of peoples is preserved in their indifference to the
stabilisation of finite institutions; just as the blowing of the winds
preserves the sea from the foulness which would be the result of pro-
longed calm, so corruption in nations would be the product of pro-
longed, let alone 'perpetual', peace.

Unrelieved peace is bad, on this view, because it leads to ossifica-
tion and stagnation in society, war good because it stirs things up
and so injects health into the body politic. Peace again fosters

individualism, the exclusive concern with private enrichment and security; war has the advantage of putting a higher aim before us, the good of the community as a whole. But one suspects that the main difference between the two, from Hegel's point of view, was that in war the community was more of a genuine community, while in peace it settled down into being little more than 'the external state'. It was only in conditions of war that positive adherence to the state was unmistakably displayed.

I believe myself that it is a mistake to think that positive adherence to the state is shown only in times of war. As I have already pointed out, it is also manifested in the pride and shame which people of many kinds feel when the actions and condition of their country are in question. Positive adherence here does not entail positive approval: the man who systematically denigrates his country and denounces everything it does (the expatriate American in Europe, the expatriate Briton in America) reveals in doing so the extent to which he is bound up with it, and remains a patriot of a sort. There are few persons who are so cosmopolitan in their outlook as to have become utterly indifferent to the reputation of the land of their birth: if they no longer care about its political activities, they will remain sensitive about its standing in the world of sport, or resent criticism of its intellectual life. This of course does not mean that involvement in corporate life is equally keen in all conditions; there are periods of stagnation in the life of any community, as Hegel knew well from his personal experience (he began his youthful essay on the German constitution with the words: 'Germany is a state no longer').[61] In special circumstances individuals will become wholly estranged from the community in which they live, and will try in consequence to find satisfaction in purely private activities. But these circumstances are, despite modern journalists, fortunately rare, and the normal condition is for the state as Hegel understood it to be a living reality. It can be this, I hasten to add, without becoming a version of Hitler's Germany or even of Plato's *Republic*, as we can see by reflecting that the state in Hegel was meant to include civil society and not to supersede it. Community life does not need to be centrally directed throughout in order to be described as healthy.

Let me pass to a second and still more serious objection. If the state has the ethical qualities which Hegel ascribes to it, will this not mean that no one can properly rebel against or repudiate the morality of his own society? In a situation where what exists is taken as the standard of what is right, how can there be room for rational moral dissent? How again in these conditions can there be such a thing as moral improvement or moral deterioration? Shall we not have to say that moral values may change in the course of time, but that the change can be neither progression nor regression, since at each stage the prevailing practices are defined as right? Thus if slavery is an established institution in a society, it cannot be properly criticised as immoral. The possibility of challenging it will arise only when some individual slave-owners begin to liberate their slaves and so set up an alternative way of proceeding.

That Hegel recognised the facts which lie behind these questions is not in doubt: in practice, he was by no means disposed to treat all societies as morally equal. I will mention three pieces of evidence which support this interpretation. First, in *Philosophy of Right*, § 153, Hegel quotes with approval the story told in Diogenes Laertius of the father who enquired about the best way to educate his son in moral matters and was given the answer 'Make him a citizen of a state with good laws'; the clear implication here is that states can be morally inferior and superior. Secondly, in *Encyclopaedia*, § 552, in the course of a lively if not unprejudiced discussion of Catholicism and its bearing on politics, we find Hegel referring explicitly to 'governments which are bound up with institutions founded on the bondage of the spirit . . . with institutions that embody injustice and with a morally corrupt and barbaric state of society'. Such governments survive by fostering 'fanaticism',[62] a policy which can succeed only so long as they 'remain sunk in the thraldom of injustice and immorality';[63] the states in which they are found are characterised by 'externalism and dismemberment induced by a false religion',[64] a situation against which the free spirit will naturally rebel. It is scarcely to be expected that a liberal-minded man would feel the 'underlying essence' of such a community to be 'his very own being',[65] which is what happens, according to Hegel, when 'the consciously free substance . . . has actuality as the spirit of a nation'.[66] Finally there is the case of Socrates, treated most fully in Hegel's lectures on the history of philosophy. We learn there that Socrates lived in a period when the existing moral order was under severe criticism from the Sophists, with the result that general uncertainty prevailed about what was right and wrong. At this point of turning from 'natural' to 'reflective' morality:

> The State has lost its power, which consisted in the unbroken continuity of the universal spirit, as formed of single individuals, so that the individual consciousness knew no other content and reality than law. Morals have become shaken, because we have the idea present that man creates his maxims for himself. The fact that the individual comes to care for his own morality means that he becomes reflectively moral; when public morality disappears, reflective morality is seen to have arisen. We now see Socrates bringing forward the opinion, that in these times everyone has to look after his own morality, and thus he looked after his through consciousness and reflection regarding himself; for he sought the universal spirit which had disappeared from reality in his own consciousness.[67]

An understanding of this situation enables us to see why Socrates suffered the fate he did, but it also makes clear that his was a higher morality than the traditional morality of his accusers.

Hegel's official answer to the charge that it is quite inconsistent of him to talk in these terms is that it leaves out of account the all-important fact that his theory of morals culminates in a philosophy of history. It is possible to speak of one society as being more advanced morally than another because it is possible to see history as a general, if not exactly unbroken, progress in the consciousness and realisation of freedom. What happens at any stage in this progress is necessarily what it is, yet that does not prevent there being a development from one stage to another. Thus the morality of the Greek world before the time of the Sophists was inferior to that of the Christian world, because it allowed no scope for individual judgment; once the Sophists had suggested that morals might be man-made rather than god-given, the old system according to which customary moral principles had the ineluctable necessity of laws of nature became outmoded. But the particularism of the Christian world had its drawbacks too: it failed to embody the universal or impersonal element which was so prominent in the system it overthrew. Hence the transition to the modern system, which combines objectivity with subjectivity, and allows the individual liberty to subscribe to his own moral principles without sacrificing universality on the altar of personal caprice.

That history is to be seen as progress in the consciousness and realisation of freedom is thought by Hegel to follow from premises which are partly philosophical, partly empirical. The philosophical premises in question are supplied by Hegel's writings on logic, which offer an abstract account of the self-development of spirit and of its necessary embodiment in the world of concrete actuality. I shall make no attempt to discuss this account now; it is enough in the present context to point out that, even if it is agreed that spirit must develop in this way, nothing follows about the desirability of the process. As Hegel himself insisted (see Section IV, above), logic alone cannot establish any value judgment. The empirical premises to which Hegel makes appeal in this context are just the ordinary facts of history: unprejudiced scrutiny of these will, it is claimed, show that the course of history is as Hegel describes it, at least to the man who has mastered the general Hegelian outlook. But even if this claim is granted, important questions bearing on the legitimacy of moral dissent remain.

Consider in this connection the two cases referred to above: the change that was introduced into Greek moral life by the Sophists, and the state of affairs in Catholic countries in Europe in Hegel's own lifetime. Hegel shows considerable historical acuteness over the first of these, both in fastening on to the new principle which was making its appearance on the ethical scene at the time and in discerning the different reactions to it of Socrates and Plato (Socrates tried to meet it by giving morality a new 'reflective' dimension; Plato thought it could be dealt with only by reaffirming that private judgment has no rights in the moral sphere whatsoever). But he does not discuss the question whether those who insisted on the new principle were right to do so; his attitude is rather that, because it succeeded in getting itself accepted, it must have been right. If this is so, Aristophanes' defence of the morality of the men who fought at Marathon must be dismissed as a failure. But the only ground Hegel can offer in support of such a dismissal is that Aristophanes and those who thought like him were outmoded; they had failed to see which way the moral wind was blowing. Similarly in the case of the barbaric practices of Catholic Europe in the early nineteenth century. What was wrong with these countries, from Hegel's point of view, was broadly that they had failed to come to terms with the French Revolution; their rulers did not recognise the essential correctness of the principle which the Revolution embodied. But if we ask what made that principle correct, the only answer again is that it was widely adopted at the time, and showed promise of gaining even wider support. The Catholic states of Europe were barbaric precisely because they were backward; their rulers, and perhaps even their inhabitants, showed a deplorable tendency to turn a blind eye to advances in modern thought.

To make his case good Hegel must show not just that there is a discernible line of development in history (a Metternich or a de Maistre might dispute the correctness of the line he offers), but further that the later stages in any such development are, in general, superior to the earlier. Failing this he has nothing pertinent to say on really fundamental moral disputes. Like his follower Bradley he can make allowance for a limited kind of internal moral reform, the sort that is involved in straightening out inconsistencies or extending the application of principles which are already accepted. But when asked to adjudicate in a clash between one whole moral way of life and another – say, that followed in Skye under the guidance of Free Church ministers and that followed in swinging London under the guidance of the B.B.C. – he is not in a position to pronounce. He can say only that one code holds in Skye and another in London; he may judge that the one or the other will gain the upper hand, but he certainly cannot say which ought to. And this is because, as we argued at the beginning, his ethical theory, if carried to its logical conclusion, involves the dissolution of ethics in sociology. Only the dubious doctrine that world history is the world court concealed this important conclusion from Hegel himself.

We have still to deal with a further criticism which on the face of things is even harder for Hegel to meet. We have seen that he has a good deal to say about the need for a 'universal' element in morality, by which he apparently means its being free from individual caprice. But it could be argued with some force that his theory precludes any genuinely universal morality, just because it ties morality so closely to the nation state. Concrete ethics as he expounds it is part of the life of a national community, and no national community is all-embracing. It follows that, despite certain liberal elements in his theory, Hegel is advocating a closed rather than an open morality. If he is to be consistent he must demand that the moral agent be actuated by the thought of the good of the fellow-members of his group rather than that of men as men. He must stress virtues like loyalty and patriotism which rest on principles which cannot be universalised just because they involve a particular reference. And if he does that he faces the charge of being a moral reactionary, whose theories cannot expect to get serious consideration from civilised persons.

Unfortunately Hegel offers no explicit discussion of the issues here involved. Despite his interest in the varieties of the moral life, he has no clear grasp of the difference between open and closed morality. There are places in which he seems to accept the principle that human beings are entitled to consideration in virtue of their humanity, as in the following passage from the section on civil society:

It is part of education, of thinking as the consciousness of the single in the form of universality, that the ego comes to be apprehended as a universal person in which all are identical. A man counts as a man in virtue of his manhood alone, not because he is a Jew, Catholic, Protestant, German, Italian, etc. This is an assertion which thinking ratifies and to be conscious of it is of infinite importance.[68]

E

But the effect of this is immediately cancelled by the next sentence:

It is defective only when it is crystallised, e.g. as a cosmopolitanism in opposition to the concrete life of the state.

It is not clear exactly what Hegel is here denouncing as 'cosmopolitanism'. Is it what he would regard as sentimental interference in the affairs of other countries, based on appeal to fundamental 'human' rights? Or is it the demand that the moral traditions and practices of one's own community be subject to scrutiny in the light of a universal morality? If the first alternative is correct Hegel could defend himself by pointing out that protests of this sort more often than not fall on deaf ears, and do so precisely because the values of a living community carry more weight with those primarily concerned than any abstract principle. The situation has certainly changed since Hegel's day, thanks to the growth of an international public opinion which individual nations seek to use in their own interests, but it could be argued that it remains unaltered in essentials. If, however, the term 'cosmopolitanism' is taken to cover the appeal to a universal morality against the moral traditions of one's own society, some argument must be produced in favour of the position Hegel takes up, and so far as I can see none is forthcoming. Hegel would be correct if he confined himself to the modest point that it is not self-evident that a moral system must be universalistic after the Kantian fashion; the morality of the closed society is far from dead even now, nor is its incidence confined to communities and groups which are backward, as can be seen by considering contemporary Russia and China, to say nothing of the British working class. It would be correct, again, to emphasise that, in conditions where group consciousness is enhanced, as for instance in the Turkish and Greek communities in Cyprus today, universal morality has little or no appeal. But none of this shows that there is no case for it whatsoever. Nor could it be said that it is merely an empty ideal, not a reality. People may pay less attention to its precepts than they would like to think, but it remains true that those precepts have force in some degree. They have gained embodiment in everyday moral life, and that should entitle them to respect from Hegel as a moral philosopher.

The most that can be said for Hegel on this point is that he has drawn attention forcibly to an important feature of the moral situation about which Kant, for reasons discussed already (Section III), was silent. Hegel saw that moral behaviour is a part of community life just as polite behaviour or legal behaviour is: morals can no more be taken in abstraction from a particular society than can manners or law. All three in fact serve the same general social purpose, to bring pressure to bear on the individual so that he acts for the public good. But the value of this insight was diminished by two accompanying defects. First, Hegel paid insufficient attention to the universal aspect of morality, in the way we have just seen. His contempt for the shallow cosmopolitanism of the eighteenth century, which connected in his opinion with a wholly inadequate grasp of the nature of the state, goes some way to explain his attitude. Secondly and more seriously, he failed to notice that a man can belong to more communities than one, and that this fact is important when it comes to considering the moral life. It is not true that the latter is a seamless web, or that the state automatically has authority against any sub-groups which operate within it. Hegel was perhaps right to believe that national sentiment will normally prevail over class loyalties or religious affiliations, but he had no justification for assuming that this will always happen. His opinions on this subject were too much coloured by his own experience to be truly enlightening. Nor did he explore as he might have done the possibility that there might develop a common moral consciousness which was supranational without being cosmopolitan: one shared by all Europeans, for example, or again by all black Africans. He assumed too readily that the history of the world would go on being the history of particular peoples just because it had done so up to his own time.

The argument that Hegel neglected the more personal aspects of morality has already been considered above (Section III). The probabilities are that he always meant to leave room for what might be called cultivation of the individual soul, but saw the primary concern of ethics as being with men's interpersonal transactions. An impatience with mere conscientiousness, the pursuit of the good will as an end in itself (compare on this the passage on 'the beautiful soul' in the *Phenomenology*), doubtless reinforced this attitude of his. In my opinion he was entirely right to take such a view. But I shall not attempt to argue further in support of this judgment now.

I propose to conclude this brief survey of Hegel's ethical opinions by examining some aspects of his moral psychology. This is a difficult subject, if only because Hegel is much less explicit about it than he might have been. In much of the *Philosophy of Right* he uses Kantian language, and in particular seems to retain the concept of duty in the privileged position Kant assigned to it. But we have seen above (especially in Sections V and VI) that he thought there were radical defects in Kant's picture of the moral situation. The Kantian antithesis of reason and inclination was much too sharp; it was not true to say that we could act rationally only if we could subdue our animal impulses, nor that any activity which was prompted by inclination must be mechanically determined. An altogether different account of the position must be given.

In 'The Spirit of Christianity' Hegel made use of the Aristotelian concept of virtue and of the notion of love in an attempt to construct such an account. A man who possesses a virtue has a settled disposition to act in a certain way; he is not all the time struggling with counter-inclinations. And a man who is actuated by love does what he does with what I previously called open-hearted sympathy; he feels the distress of others and does not need to invoke respect for the moral law in order to set himself to relieve it. Love as so expounded plays a part not unlike that of sympathy in Hume's ethics, though it is obvious that Hegel took the idea not from any philosopher but from the New Testament. Despite this resemblance, however, it seems extremely unlikely that Hegel had serious thoughts, even at this stage, of explaining moral behaviour in terms of a psychological mechanism. In his mature philosophy he expressed contempt for the kind of ethical theory which had prevailed before Kant:

To estimate rightly what we owe to Kant in the matter, we ought to set before our minds the form of practical philosophy and in particular of 'moral philosophy' which prevailed in his time. It may be generally described as a system of Eudaemonism, which, when asked what man's chief end ought to be, replied Happiness. And by happiness Eudaemonism understood the satisfaction of the private appetites, wishes and wants of the man: thus raising the contingent and particular into a principle for the will and its actualisation. To this Eudaemonism, which was destitute of stability and consistency, and which left the 'door and gate' wide open for every whim and caprice, Kant opposed the practical reason, and thus emphasised the need for a principle of will which should be universal and lay the same obligation on all.[69]

This passage does not suggest that Hegel could ever have been content with the idea that reason is and ought only to be the slave of the private passions, even when it is added that the passions at their best operate under the control of a principle of sympathy.

The question is, however, what alternative role Hegel can find for reason to play, and this question is the more urgent when we remember Hegel's criticisms (above, Section IV) of the function which Kant had assigned to it. The answer, I believe, is on the following lines. The basic fact about human beings – the fact which differentiates them from everything else in the world – is that they can think and be conscious of their thoughts. This means that they are not, as animals presumably are, at the mercy of their particular impulses, but can pursue purposes. A purposive being is able to postpone immediate satisfactions in order to seek a goal whose attainment will be more satisfying in the long run. But this must not be interpreted as meaning that such a being is dominated by a master passion which blots out all other impulses. The truth is rather that he has an idea, however inexact, of his welfare as a whole, and that it is this idea which shapes his conduct. He is not a creature of impulses which has the good fortune to possess an instrument for their effective realisation, but a being whose impulsive life is transformed by the fact that he can think.

So far this perhaps suggests a view not unlike that of Butler with his principle of self-love. But Hegel differs from Butler in important respects (and incidentally does not even mention him in his lectures on the history of philosophy). For one thing, Butler leaves the particular propensities, as he calls them, standing along-side his more general principle; he takes the view that men can be actuated by self-love, but will quite often give way to un-restrained impulse. For Hegel, by contrast, men are never at the mercy of simple impulse; their whole orectic life is altered funda-mentally by the presence of thought. And there is a second and even more important difference. When Butler spoke of self-love he was thinking, as other philosophers of his time did, of the self as an isolated unit, complete in itself. But Hegel, as we have had occasion to notice more than once in the foregoing pages, re-jected this conception of the self decisively. In his opinion no one had or could have a purely private self. I owe my thoughts, aspirations and even feelings to others as much as to myself; they connect with, and must be seen against the background of, a set of traditions, and traditions are unintelligible without reference to society. There is thus a sense in which the pursuit of my own welfare is not the pursuit of a purely private goal.

But society comes into my activities in other ways besides this. Many of my aims are such as to be unrealisable without the active co-operation or passive acquiescence of others; I could not, for example, provide for my old age through savings or insurance unless I could count on relative financial stability in the country I live in and some measure of legal protection for property. And others owe their very existence to the fact that I am engaged with my fellows in a variety of enterprises and look on myself as be-longing with them to a wider whole. I could not have a passionate desire to see the standing of my country improved unless this were true. I might in these conditions have other desires, but I certainly could not have this particular one, or anything like it. The position here is, in fact, parallel to that we discussed above in expounding the Hegelian doctrine of the family. Just as there are certain satisfactions which are possible only within the institution of marriage, so there are others which are possible only within the state. And to describe the attainment of such satisfactions, in the one case or the other, as a matter of purely personal pleasure is at least misleading. I want my country to succeed, and shall be pleased if it does, but this will be pleasure in a common success, not a private satisfaction of my own.

If the above argument is correct, reason as Hegel understands it is by no means exclusively concerned with the welfare of the individual in the narrow sense of that term. Thought makes the pursuit of purposes possible, and every purpose is, of course, someone's purpose. But it does not follow from this that every purpose must be looked on as selfish, for some, as we have seen, require the co-operation of other people, while others are impossible except within the context of a joint enterprise. A concern with welfare thus passes naturally from a private to a public stage; the good it has in mind may start as my good in the private sense, but widens to include first the good of all my associates (as when I participate in business activities) and then the common good of the community at large. However this theory should be described, it is not a species of vulgar egoism.

It may be useful at this point to try to connect Hegel's account of reason with his doctrine of freedom, for the terms 'free' and 'rational' are often juxtaposed in his vocabulary. Common thought, he argued, takes being free as being able to exercise the arbitrary will; a man is free on this view if he can do what he wants, whatever that may be. But this, said Hegel, involved a profound mistake, for volition is a matter of content as well as form, and 'arbitrariness implies that the content is made mine not by the nature of my will but by chance'.[70] In exercising my arbitrary will I may do what I want in the formal sense of doing the action that I most prefer among the available alternatives, but this does not give me any control over what possibilities are open to me. To be free in the full sense is to be fully self-determining, which means that one is not at the mercy either of external circumstances or of uncontrollable internal forces. Hegel argued that this condition could be achieved only if men were ready to put aside purely individual demands and to identify themselves with rational and universal purposes, i.e. engage in enterprises in which what counted was not personal self-assertion but the result to be brought about or the activity itself. To put the argument in his own words:

The man in the street thinks he is free if it is open to him to act as he pleases, but his very arbitrariness implies that he is not free. When I will what is rational, then I am acting not as a particular individual but in accordance with the concepts of ethics in general. In an ethical action, what I vindicate is not myself but the thing. But in doing a perverse action, it is my singularity which I bring to the centre of the stage. The rational is the high road where everyone travels, where no one is conspicuous. When great artists complete a masterpiece, we speak of its inevitability, which means that the artist's idiosyncrasy has completely disappeared and no mannerism is detectable in it. Pheidias has no mannerisms; his figures themselves live and declare themselves. But the worse the artist is, the more we see in his work the artist, his singularity, his arbitrariness.[71]

There can be no doubt of the correctness of the general point which is made here. There is a wide range of human activities, as Plato already made clear in the first book of the *Republic*, which require those who engage in them to suppress their private personalities and adhere to rules which hold without distinction of persons; acceptance of such rules is none the less not thought of as constricting. The mathematician who thinks in accordance with the principles of his science is more, not less, free than his colleague who breaks with them just because he wishes to be different. As Plato said,[72] one good musician will not try to outdo another: the way he plays will be determined by the demands of his art, yet he will not feel that these are imposed on him by some alien power. The interesting question is, however, whether Hegel is right in supposing that the same sort of thing can be said about ethics. The reply to this turns, I suggest, on how we answer two further questions. First, have we reason to assume that engaging in the moral life is engaging in an enterprise directed to an end? Is practising morality practising an art in the Platonic understanding of that term? And secondly, could it be fairly claimed that the position of the moral agent is similar to that of the mathematician and the musician in the examples just cited; that just as the latter feels himself quite free in accepting the rules of his art or science, so the former will, in general, feel quite free in accepting the rules of morality?

I do not know if Hegel anywhere discusses the first point

explicitly, but it seems to me at least plausible to suggest that he thought of the moral life as an enterprise directed to an end, just as Plato and Aristotle did. The end in question was human welfare as understood in particular societies; behaving morally promoted it both negatively by removing conditions, e.g. unrestrained indulgence in sensual pleasures, which prevented its realisation, and positively in supplying opportunities for valuable co-operative activity. By taking his place in society and fulfilling the duties which that involved a man at once suppressed the side of his nature which threatened to render all his actions ineffective and widened the range of his own possible satisfactions, in the way we have outlined above. It could thus be said that moral requirements were not the alien restraints they are commonly taken to be, but rather something the acceptance of which was rational in a familiar sense of the term: rational because it conduced to, and indeed was an indispensable condition of the attainment of, a good which men really want. To describe that good as their own, as Plato and Aristotle did, was misleading, in so far as it suggested that they were seeking no more than their private happiness. We have seen already what Hegel thought of such vulgar Eudaemonism. But that did not mean that the notion of 'the good for man' could be set aside as irrelevant to moral conduct, as Kant had in effect argued. If we abandoned the common assumption that man is a purely private being and recognised his fundamentally social character, it could be put to a very good use.

Even if this is correct as an interpretation of Hegel's position, it remains to justify the position on philosophical grounds. It would be idle to deny that to accept any such account of the moral 'enterprise' involves abandoning some of the central distinctions of modern moral philosophy. If morality is an institution aimed at an end, namely human welfare, we cannot draw the sharp contrast which Prichard did between duty and interest, nor can we follow Kant in distinguishing laws of morality, which command categorically, from counsels of prudence, which have only hypothetical force. The question, 'Why should I be moral?', declared by many writers on ethics to be totally illegitimate, will after all have an answer: I should be moral because I cannot attain what I really want without being so. But it should be added here that what I want is not just personal satisfaction in the narrow sense, as old-fashioned advocates of this kind of position were apt to think. Since I exist, as it were, in intimate union with my fellows, owing my whole mind and outlook as much to them as to myself, the good in which I am interested is not a narrowly personal good. To use Bradley's language, I aspire to realise myself in what ever I do, but cannot forward my own aims without forwarding those of others. Sustained action, whether on my part or theirs, is possible only if we co-operate; morality, like law, is a device which serves to make co-operation possible by discouraging conduct which is disruptive because immediately egoistic. And the justification for accepting its restraints is that by so doing we are put in a position to live an altogether richer life, one which includes satisfactions that would be entirely beyond our reach if we lived, *per impossibile*, each in a private world of his own.

To argue properly in favour of this view would be an extensive undertaking; here I can say only that it seems to me to deserve altogether more serious consideration than it has had in recent years. It has the advantage of treating morality as an intelligible activity which performs a social purpose, instead of as a mysterious phenomenon to be explained in non-natural terms. It is also strong in connecting moral behaviour with the satisfaction of human wants and the pursuit of human good, rather than with the demands of a law which is not human at all. It makes the same claim to be realistic as common Utilitarianism, but avoids the psychological and sociological simplicities on which most versions of Utilitarianism are based.

Yet the view is not free of difficulties, at least in the form in which we are ascribing it to Hegel. I said above (p. 64) that the end to which the moral enterprise is directed in this account of the matter is human welfare *as understood in particular societies*. The qualifying words here need emphasis, for it goes without saying that societies vary in their styles of living, both in comparison with each other and at different times in their individual histories. They each perhaps aim at a good, but conceptions of what that good is can and do vary. And this fact has an important bearing on the second question we posed, about whether men accept the discipline of morality as readily as, for example, doctors accept the discipline of medicine and mathematicians that of mathematics. It would need a bold man to say that they always do. But their failure to do so need not be taken as proof that morality is something other than a necessary condition of what we really want; it can be explained by reference to the feeling they have of being estranged from their particular society. The moral rules of a community in general facilitate a common life of which most members of the community may be expected to approve, but that does not prevent there being persons in the society who for one reason or another are out of sympathy with the prevailing view, and who accordingly find those rules irksome and alien. In every society there are sub-societies whose members favour a style of life which diverges at important points from that which is accepted by the majority; some of these look backward to the past, others claim to herald the future. It is natural in these conditions that the prevailing moral procedures should strike some as an instrument of oppression rather than liberation, a structure which is arbitrary as opposed to rational and one they accept only because and so far as they must.

In his lectures on the philosophy of history Hegel had a good deal to say about the shifting character of human societies; he also laid stress there on the way in which a new society begins to develop inside one which is in decline. He showed particular interest in the break-up of the unreflective ethical world of early Greece, and again in the circumstances in which Christianity triumphed over paganism. It is therefore all the more surprising that he made no allowance for moral variation in his ethical theory. That he did not do so is to be connected, I think, with the highly abstract character of his account of the moral life. What he called 'the philosophic science of the state' was concerned, in his opinion, with the notion of the state rather than with its historical manifestations; particular states might diverge from the concept in all sorts of important ways, but it remained the philosopher's task to concentrate on what the state really is, which means thinking out what being a state would be if conditions were ideal.[73] We have seen already that Hegel differentiated this activity sharply from that of sketching a utopia: the theory set out in the *Philosophy of Right* was, he argued, firmly founded in fact, just as Plato's picture of the republic was rooted in the historical conditions of Greek life. The philosopher had to grasp the essence of the state, not to make it up, and it was essential to the state that it should be 'the actuality of concrete freedom',[74] 'the actuality of the ethical Idea',[75] 'absolutely rational inasmuch as it is the actuality of the substantial will which it possesses in the particular self-consciousness once that consciousness has been raised to consciousness of its universality'.[76]

But it remains difficult to reconcile these bold words with Hegel's recognition elsewhere of diversity and disruption within particular societies. There are occasions, perhaps, on which a state is something like the unity in diversity which Hegel takes it to be; there are others when it emphatically is not. The Hegelian idea of a common life in which all or most citizens share certainly has a wider application than is recognised by philosophers of an individualist turn of mind; Hegel's strictures[77] on the confusion of the state with civil society, and his polemic against belief in the atomic individual, are amply justified. But it is possible to avoid the extremes of individualism without agreeing that there is only one whole in which a man can realise his full potentialities: that constituted by the state or nation. There are lesser wholes within the state; there are also unities which are supranational if not fully international. And these facts have, or can have, an important bearing on the moral attitudes of particular individuals. Hegel should certainly have taken account of them.

Hegel's writings on ethics and politics are an object of suspicion to many liberal-minded persons because of their supposed totalitarian tendencies; to suggest, as I have, that his moral psychology commits him to denying any absolute distinction between duty and expediency can only increase that suspicion. It is therefore worth noting by way of appendix to this discussion that in practice Hegel laid great stress on personal rights and responsibilities; he was not disposed to argue that it did not matter how people were treated so long as it was for the good of the

67

community generally. This comes out nowhere more clearly than in his celebrated doctrine of punishment, to which I can make only the briefest of references here. Punishment, says Hegel, can be understood only if we see it in a context of rights. We must not look on it as an evil irrationally added to the evil of the crime, or even as a good which cancels out the latter. It is rather the righting of a wrong, and as such is 'inherently and actually just'.[78] Nor is the injured party the only one whose rights are in question: the criminal too has his rights in the matter – 'by being punished he is honoured as a rational being'.[79] As Hegel explains

his action is the action of a rational being and this implies that it is something universal and that by doing it the criminal has laid down a law which he has explicitly recognised in his action and under which in consequence he should be brought as under his right.[80]

I take this to mean that the criminal knows what he is doing and so commits himself to accepting the consequences of his act, including punishment if his crime is detected. To treat him 'either as a harmful animal who has to be made harmless, or with a view to deterring and reforming him'[81] is to leave out the all-important fact that he is a responsible agent. That men are such agents and must be treated as such is a central tenet in all Hegel's thinking about ethics. However much he sought to correct or develop Kant, he had no doubt that Kant was right over this particular point.

X. THE BRITISH HEGELIANS

I have taken the title 'Hegelian ethics' to refer to the ethics of Hegel himself rather than to a general view which derives from Hegel. Part of my reason for so doing was that I wanted to try to fill an obvious gap in philosophical literature, little or nothing having been written from a modern point of view on this aspect of Hegel's work. But I also think that it can be fairly claimed that, in ethics at any rate, Hegel stands head and shoulders above those who followed him in everything except literary skill, and thus that his theories deserve independent philosophical consideration as those of later Hegelians do not. The ethical opinions of Green, Bradley and Bosanquet are certainly not uninteresting; despite the low repute in which Green and Bosanquet stand today there is something to be learned from all three of them. But their most distinctive doctrines, as they would themselves have been the first to acknowledge, are derivative, and the main source from which they drew them was Hegel. These writers are, in general, more lucid than Hegel and more easily understood, but they are also, unfortunately, more provincial in their outlook and less profound in their ethical insights. Their thought is for the most part free of the extravagances and eccentricities which mar Hegel's wilder pronouncements, but equally it lacks the penetration and originality which are the other side of the Hegelian coin.

I shall now attempt to document and support these judgments. In a review published in 1880 T. H. Green wrote:

That there is one spiritual self-conscious being, of which all that is real is the activity or expression; that we are related to this spiritual being, not merely as parts of the world which is its expression, but as partakers in some inchoate measure of the self-consciousness through which it at once constitutes and distinguishes itself from the world; that this participation is the source of morality and religion; this we take to be the vital truth which Hegel had to teach.[82]

Green perhaps saw his own main task in philosophy as being to present this truth 'in a form which will command some general acceptance among serious and scientific men'.[83] But in ethics at any rate what he produced was only a watered-down version of Hegelianism, as inspection of his posthumously published *Prolegomena* will show. The book begins with a restatement of some of the main metaphysical doctrines of Absolute Idealism, offered as an alternative to and refutation of then fashionable naturalistic theories. The idea that man is a purely natural object is dismissed: the fact of knowledge implies a continuing consciousness which may be materially conditioned, but cannot be materially constituted. Nor can it be claimed that men are the only non-natural beings, for nature too points beyond itself to 'a principle which is not natural':[84] as a system of things in relation it demands a subject, itself outside the system, for which the relations hold. Knowledge is possible only because of the affinity between the mind of man and the mind which stands behind, and indeed makes, nature. To rest content with a half-way position, as Kant did, making the human mind operate on material supplied by an alien source, is to shut one's eyes to the most evident impossibilities.

Having established these points to his satisfaction Green turns next to human agency and human conduct, his first object being to produce an account of the psychology of action. Human beings, unlike animals, are not mere creatures of wants. Their natural impulses are transformed by the fact that they occur in a continuing consciousness which can pursue purposes, with the result that in the world of practice the determining causes are *motives*, a motive being 'an idea of an end which a self-conscious subject presents to itself, and which it strives and tends to realise'.[85] An end of this kind is always something seen as good, and Green commits himself to the seemingly unacceptable conclusion that 'the motive in every imputable act for which the agent is conscious on reflection that he is answerable, is a desire for personal good in some form or other'.[86] But he is quick to repudiate any suggestion that this involves acquiescence in hedonism: the pursuit of happiness upon the whole is not the pursuit of a series of momentary pleasures. And he argues in the later part of his book that it is not to accept egoism either, since there is nothing to prevent an identification of my good with a good common to many persons or indeed to humanity generally.

This, however, is to anticipate. What deserves comment at this stage is the enlightened nature of Green's general account of action, when compared with the crude push-and-pull psychology it was meant to replace. In insisting that human beings are not at the mercy of their impulses as they were said to be by naturalistic philosophers, and that the satisfactions they pursue are certainly not all of a piece, Green was making a point which is still instructive. The metaphysical framework inside which he developed his moral psychology may well be dubious, but even if it is that does not invalidate the psychology itself. Green's old-fashioned language and stiff Victorian manner put a serious barrier between him and any modern reader, on this subject as elsewhere. But there are important parallels, some of them close, between his views and those expressed by a number of recent writers in the field of philosophy of mind, and we ought in consequence to try to break the barrier down, at least at this point.

Green is less successful when he comes to discuss 'the moral ideal', which constitutes the central topic of the *Prolegomena*. The good for man as he sees it turns out to be little more than the realisation in persons of good will for its own sake; it is thus largely Kantian in conception. Admittedly Green pays more attention than Kant to the fact that men develop their personalities in a social setting; as he keeps insisting, the good which has to be brought about is not merely my good but a common good. Yet his overall outlook, like Kant's, is humanitarian or cosmopolitan: he sees nothing to admire, and indeed much to suspect, in the suggestion that a state might possess moral qualities. Virtue can be realised only in persons. Similarly, though he takes up Hegel's puzzle about the gap between 'ought' and 'is' and offers a general solution of it in terms of his metaphysics (in accepting the unconditional commands of duty I am in effect identifying myself with the spiritual principle which actuates the universe), he shows no interest in Hegel's own type of solution. The reason for this is, I think, twofold. First, Green shared

Hegel's preoccupation with political and social issues, but approached them from a point of view which remained individualist despite his metaphysical convictions. He derived his individualism from evangelical Christianity, which he also admired for its insistence on the sense of sin. Secondly, Green lacked Hegel's acute historical insight, his feeling for the points of difference between one age and community and another. Green has a good deal to say about the development of the moral ideal, but the very fact that he speaks of it in the singular betrays his superficiality. The extent of real moral diversity escapes him. As a result he produces an ethical system which certainly falls in the Hegelian mould, but is far less interesting in its details than that of Hegel himself.

Green was perhaps never more than a doubting Hegelian; F. H. Bradley, whose *Ethical Studies* appeared seven years before Green's *Prolegomena* in 1876, was at this early stage of his career far more openly committed to Hegel. Bradley does not merely borrow particular Hegelian arguments in criticising his opponents, for example when he maintains (*Ethical Studies*, pp. 97–8) that the Utilitarian ideal is impossible because it rests on the self-contradictory notion of a completable sum of pleasures; he speaks in Hegelian accents throughout his book. And he sets out his whole argument in Hegelian style, by first exposing sharply the shortcomings of a pair of diametrically opposed positions, and then offering a theory which purports to retain all that is valuable in each while excising its defects. Moreover, he begins the constructive side of his task with a brilliantly persuasive and perceptive account of Hegel's ethics in the shape of the celebrated essay on 'My Station and its Duties', an essay which leaves the reader in no doubt that Bradley's main sympathies were with Hegel. Bradley was certainly not an uncritical supporter of the notion of 'concrete ethics': he went out of his way in the course of his exposition to point out that though 'systems and institutions, from the family to the nation' constitute 'the body of the moral world',[87] they are nothing without the willing acquiescence of persons. For him, as indeed for Hegel himself, it is in the hearts and minds of persons that morality really lives; he is far from ascribing moral authority to a mere institution as such. But he also insists, correctly as it seems to me, that to isolate the individual from his social connections and make him the sole centre of moral interest as an autonomous moral agent is in general quite mistaken. There *is* a sphere of 'ideal morality' which supervenes on the morality of 'my station and its duties', but there can be no question of substituting the former for the latter. Bradley is in a way aware that there are higher claims on a man than narrowly moral claims, but he rightly refuses to accord them exclusive importance, or to dismiss 'conventional' morality in favour of a concern with personal salvation or personal purity of heart. He shared an evangelical background with Green, but emancipated himself from it as Green never did.

Yet for all this Bradley's standpoint in ethics is only partially Hegelian. He recognises and emphasises the social setting of the moral life, but he is not interested as Hegel is in its details. What preoccupies him most is the question how the moral agent can be said to 'realise himself' in behaving morally; to what extent in shedding his 'bad self' and identifying himself with something 'universal' he is involved not so much in self-fulfilment as in a kind of self-sacrifice. These are themes which would have excited Hegel's interest, but they are not the matters about which he has most to say as a moral philosopher. And if we ask what explains this divergence between Hegel and his admirer, the answer must again be that Hegel had a breadth of historical knowledge and depth of historical insight which Bradley largely lacked. There was a period, immediately before he wrote *Ethical Studies*, when Bradley showed a lively interest in certain philosophical questions about history, an interest which sprang from reflection on concrete historical issues. Significantly, however, these issues concerned the historical basis of Christianity: Bradley was drawn to them by his need to make up his mind about religion. There is little or nothing in what he says either in *Ethical Studies* or elsewhere to suggest that he had any deep interest in the human past for its own sake. And without such an interest he could not be expected to develop an ethical theory on genuinely Hegelian lines. *Ethical Studies* remains one of the most lively works on its subject in the English language; its chapter on 'My Station and its

Duties' still constitutes by far the best introduction to Hegelian ideas about ethics. Yet it should be pointed out (and Bradley himself would certainly endorse this view) that it is at best only a partial introduction to that subject: there are many features of Hegel's thought in this field which Bradley passes over in silence, and there are topics he discusses on which Hegel has nothing to say.

Of the three major English Idealists Bernard Bosanquet is generally reckoned to have been closest to Hegel. Green, as we have seen, had an ethical outlook which was more Kantian than Hegelian; he recognised the shortcomings of ethical individualism, but continued in some respects to work within its assumptions. Bradley when he wrote *Ethical Studies* had no such reservations, but his writings on logic and metaphysics (*Principles of Logic*, 1883; *Appearance and Reality*, 1893) were to reveal serious doubts about the tenability of Hegel's main doctrines. His thought in his mature philosophy was much more sceptical than constructive. But Bosanquet was convinced that Hegel had got things right, as regards essentials, in logic and metaphysics and ethics alike. Hegel was not the sole contributor to what Bosanquet innocently called 'the theory of the State'. That theory, he wrote,

is primarily the outcome of Greek life and thought, and has found its most congenial soil in English and American experience. It is true that a great genius in Germany was beforehand with us in appreciating Greek political ideas and in divining those which English life was destined to intensify. But their further growth is due to thinkers versed in Anglo-Saxon self-government, or inspired by the Italian risorgimento.[88]

Despite these disclaimers, Bosanquet's *Philosophical Theory of the State* is very much an Hegelian book, at least in its main outlines. It reproduces more of the content of the *Philosophy of Right* than either Green or Bradley, and it reproduces it with more enthusiasm. Bosanquet was under no illusions about the unreality of what he called 'the separate, or would-be separate, human person'[89] – the atomic individual of the theories of his opponents. He saw nothing derogatory in acknowledging that we are each in debt to society in a way which can never be paid: we could not be

74

ourselves without incurring and retaining such debts. Yet Bosanquet is far from drawing collectivist conclusions from this picture of the situation. He is never tired of emphasising that moral effort must be made by individual agents: the state or society cannot actively promote the good life, but only hinder hindrances to it. To quote a typical passage:

The State is in its right when it forcibly hinders a hindrance to the best life or common good. In hindering such hindrances it will indeed do positive acts. It may try to hinder illiteracy and intemperance by compelling education and municipalising the liquor traffic. Why not, it will be asked, hinder also unemployment by universal employment, and immorality by punishing immoral and rewarding moral actions? Here comes the value of remembering that, according to our principle, State action is negative in its immediate bearing, though positive both in its actual doings and its ultimate purpose. On every problem the question must recur, 'Is the proposed measure *bona fide* confined to hindering a hindrance, or is it attempting direct promotion of the common good by force?'. For it is to be borne in mind throughout that whatever acts are enforced are, so far as the force operates, withdrawn from the higher life. The promotion of morality by force, for instance, is an absolute self-contradiction.[90]

Bosanquet compares an enforced morality to an enforced religion which, he says in a footnote, is indistinguishable from no religion at all. But in both cases he surely overestimates the importance of personal decision and explicit consent. As he says elsewhere, society affects men not only through its overt acts but also through the force of habit; through tradition if we want a politer way of putting it. We often behave well neither because we have chosen to do so nor yet because we have been forced into it, but because we had the good fortune to be brought up in that way and continue unthinkingly on the same lines. Clearly Bosanquet was wrong in the sphere of practical politics to look to people's voluntary efforts as the main if not the only source of reform. But from the point of view of his theory he was wrong in a more serious way: he did not see the contradiction between adopting the Hegelian standpoint and continuing to lay stress on individual will. It is arguable that Hegel too failed to draw this lesson properly, for he also speaks as if explicit acceptance of an action by the agent were a necessary condition of its having any virtue. The truth is rather that what comes first is the need for decent behaviour, from whatever motive. If we can get men to act rightly from good motives, so much the better. But if they have to be cajoled or badgered or merely lulled into behaving well, that is not to be despised completely. It is better that people should do the right thing for a neutral or even a wrong reason than that they should not do it at all.

There are many points in Bosanquet's *Philosophical Theory of the State* which make it worth re-reading today; in particular, it states the case against anarchic individualism in an unanswerable way. Unfortunately, it is not likely to find many readers, for much of its content is parochial and all of its writing is dull. Bosanquet had none of the sparkle of Bradley and little of the penetration of Hegel. But he had a better grasp of the structure of the moral life than most of those who have written on moral philosophy since his time.

XI. CONCLUSION

I end by restating briefly what I take to be the main lessons of Hegelian ethics.

First, there is the point throughout insisted on that morality is primarily a social rather than a personal phenomenon, something which can be understood only if we see the individual as part of a wider whole or a series of wider wholes. Personal morality – the cultivation of the pure heart for its own sake or, in Bradley's terms, the attempt on the part of the individual to be 'better than his world' – is by no means impossible and certainly not unimportant, but it is emphatically not the whole of morality. The moral life is first and foremost a corporate life lived in a community, and there is a sense in which no community can afford to allow its individual members absolute liberty of choice on whether to accept or reject prevailing moral rules. Moral rules are man-made and they are capable of being altered, but they are not made by individual men and they are not, in general, alterable by individual effort: only a group can institute a new moral practice. It follows that personal choice and decision have less importance in the moral sphere than many recent moral philosophers have supposed. There can be no question of my choosing my morality in any literal sense, and while I am morally accountable only for my voluntary actions, there are many things I do voluntarily which are not preceded by a deliberate decision on my part. Nor is it true that in ethics everything turns on the agent's intention, for the moral philosopher must fix his attention on performance as well: morality cannot be a going concern unless people *act* rightly. It is certainly a mistake to think that purity of intention or sincerity can render conduct of any kind morally legitimate: good will may be admirable, but it can also be a source of evil. Or as Hegel himself put it in a passage already quoted:

Conscience is . . . subject to the judgment of its truth or falsity, and when it appeals only to itself for a decision, it is directly at variance with what it wishes to be, namely the rule for a mode of conduct which is rational, absolutely valid, and universal.[91]

A second ethical lesson Hegel had to teach goes closely with the first. It is that moral conduct is not, as Kant supposed, the external manifestation of something godlike in man, but a type of behaviour which serves a purpose connecting with men's natural wants and inclinations. It may seem paradoxical to insist on this point, for after all Hegel is always talking about 'spirit' and implying that man is a spiritual and therefore a superior being. Hegel certainly thinks that men are superior beings, in the sense that they are not wholly at the mercy of natural forces: there are respects in which they can be said to create their own existence, as merely natural beings, sticks and stones and other animals, cannot. It is also true – and this is what lies at the centre of Hegel's idealism – that the human mind is made objective in continuing institutions, and thus that the world in which we live is to some degree penetrated by spirit. But none of this implies a commitment to supernaturalism, of the kind which it is hard to dissociate from the moral philosophy of Kant. Hegel is interested in human satisfactions and human achievements, not just in overcoming the sensual side of our nature. As I have tried to explain, he connects the possession of reason by human beings with increasing freedom from the tyranny of nature: just because they can take thought and anticipate the future men can get round obstacles and open up to themselves the possibility of achieving goods which would otherwise be entirely unknown to them. Many of these goods are social goods, attainable only as a result of co-operative activity. Yet we are not forced to conclude from these facts that men are absolutely set apart from the rest of the animal creation, still less that they have a special affinity with the author of the universe. Some later Hegelians, particularly in Britain, were inclined to draw this conclusion, but though Hegel's own language is ambiguous on the point it seems to me that he does not seriously share their attitude. Despite his overt commitment to theism, the philosophy he advocates is humanist rather than supernaturalist in its main lines.

A third instructive feature of Hegel's ethics which deserves remark is his insistence on connecting ethical reflection with awareness of moral diversity. What gives depth to Hegel's views, when we compare them with much that is written on ethics at the present day, is that Hegel has, as present-day writers have not, both a keen interest in current moral controversies and a wide historical knowledge against which to judge them. He realises, for example, that there are enormous differences as well as striking similarities between the moral world (or worlds) of the Greeks and the moral world of nineteenth-century Europe; he sees again that there were features of the moral life of the Christian middle ages which have no parallel in modern society. As a result he is able to appreciate that there is no single set of concepts which constitutes *the* concepts of ethics, no language immediately available which is *the* language of morals. There is a plurality of moral schemes and a plurality of moral points of view. I have argued earlier that Hegel fails to do justice to this feature of the ethical scene: the easy optimism of his philosophy of history prevents him from appreciating the extent to which a theory of his kind is menaced by relativism, while the historical conditions in which he lived, in a society which was homogeneous just because it was lifeless, were such that he did not see that men could have loyalties to other wholes than the state. There is a sense in which this whole side of Hegel's thinking is deeply disappointing. Yet there is another in which it can be claimed that he showed remarkable ethical grasp, pointing the way to problems which were unknown to his contemporaries and whose importance has only been partly realised by subsequent writers on the subject.

BIBLIOGRAPHY

I. Works by Hegel available in English translation

Early Theological Writings, translated by T. M. Knox and R. Kroner (Chicago, 1948). See especially pp. 205–53.

Hegel's Political Writings, translated by Sir Malcolm Knox, with introductory study by Z. A. Pelczynski (Oxford, 1964).

The Phenomenology of Mind, translated by J. B. Baillie (London, 1961; as originally published in 1910). See especially pp. 373–679.

Encyclopaedia of the Philosophical Sciences, part 3, 'The Philosophy of Mind', translated by William Wallace (Oxford, 1894). See especially pp. 240–90.

Hegel's Philosophy of Right, translated by T. M. Knox (Oxford, 1942).

Lectures on the History of Philosophy, translated by E. S. Haldane and F. H. Simson (London, 1892–5). See especially the sections on Plato's *Republic* and on Kant.

Lectures on the Philosophy of History, translated by J. Sibree (London, 1894; originally published in 1858).

II. Works on Hegel

H. A. Reyburn, *Hegel's Ethical Theory* (Oxford, 1921). Predominantly an exposition of the *Philosophy of Right*.

J. P. Plamenatz, *Man and Society* (London, 1963). See vol II, pp. 129–268; lively account of Hegel's views on morals and politics, especially politics.

J. N. Findlay, *Hegel, a Re-examination* (London, 1958). Good general account of Hegel's philosophy.

W. T. Stace, *The Philosophy of Hegel* (London, 1924). An earlier general book.

G. R. G. Mure, *The Philosophy of Hegel* (London, 1965). A brief but well-informed survey of Hegel's philosophy.

H. Marcuse, *Reason and Revolution* (London, 1941; 2nd edition, 1955). Mainly Marxist.

W. Kaufmann, *Hegel* (New York, 1965). Mostly about the connection between Hegel's ideas and his personality and early development, but with relatively little on his ethics.

H. B. Acton, 'Hegel', in the *Encyclopaedia of Philosophy*, ed. Paul Edwards (New York, 1967). A very good general introduction.

NOTES

Publication details are not given where these appear in the Bibliography.

Abbreviations

ETW Hegel, *Early Theological Writings*
PR   *Hegel's Philosophy of Right*

1. Kant, *Groundwork of the Metaphysic of Morals*, translated H. J. Paton (London, [1948]) xiii; paging from Kant's second edition.
2. *Groundwork*, 17.
3. *Groundwork*, 17.
4. *Groundwork*, 19–20.
5. *Groundwork*, 21.
6. PR preface, 12–13.
7. PR preface, 10.
8. Kant, *Groundwork*, xiv.
9. *Groundwork*, 96.
10. *Groundwork*, 95.
11. *Groundwork*, 96.
12. *Hegel's Political Writings*, 299–300.
13. *Encyclopaedia*, § 523.
14. See, for example, p. 164 in the Torchbook edition (New York, 1960).
15. PR § 185.
16. PR § 185.
17. PR § 132.
18. PR § 132.
19. PR § 137.
20. PR § 137.
21. Kant, *Groundwork*, 15 n.
22. *Groundwork*, 53.
23. PR § 135.
24. PR § 135.
25. PR § 135.
26. PR § 135.
27. *Groundwork*, 54–5.
28. *Groundwork*, 56.

29. *PR* § 135.

30. Kant, *Metaphysic of Morals*, part II, § 8.

31. Hume, *Treatise*, ed. Selby-Bigge (Oxford, 1896) 416.

32. *Treatise*, 455.

33. Hegel, *Phenomenology of Mind*, 618.

34. Kant, *Critique of Judgment*, § 87.

35. Kant, *Critique of Practical Reason*, translated L. W. Beck (Chicago, 1949) 226.

36. Hegel, *Phenomenology*, 619.

37. Ibid. 635.

38. Ibid. 636.

39. *ETW* 215 n.

40. *ETW* 214.

41. *ETW* 214.

42. *ETW* 215.

43. *ETW* 213.

44. *ETW* 212.

45. *ETW* 212.

46. *PR* § 159.

47. *PR* § 167.

48. *PR* § 162.

49. *PR* § 170.

50. *PR* § 189.

51. *PR* § 238.

52. *PR* § 243.

53. *PR* § 244.

54. *PR* § 245.

55. *PR* § 246.

56. *PR* § 248.

57. *PR* § 246.

58. *PR* § 257.

59. *PR* § 258.

60. *PR* § 324 (Hegel is quoting from his essay on natural rights, published in 1802).

61. *Hegel's Political Writings*, 143.

62. Hegel, *Encyclopaedia*, § 552.

63. *Encyclopaedia*, § 552.

64. *Encyclopaedia*, § 552.

65. *Encyclopaedia*, § 514.

66. *Encyclopaedia*, § 514.

67. Hegel, *Lectures on the History of Philosophy*, 1 409.

68. *PR* § 209.

69. *Encyclopaedia*, § 54. *The Logic of Hegel*, translated by William Wallace (Oxford, 1892).

70. *PR*, addition to § 15 (Knox translation, 230).
71. Ibid.
72. Plato, *Republic*, 349b ff.
73. *PR* § 258.
74. *PR* § 260.
75. *PR* § 257.
76. *PR* § 258.
77. *PR* § 258.
78. *PR* § 99.
79. *PR* § 100.
80. *PR* § 100.
81. *PR* § 100.
82. T. H. Green, *Works* (London, 1885–8) III 146.
83. *Works*, III 146.
84. T. H. Green, *Prolegomena to Ethics* (Oxford, 1883) § 54.
85. *Prolegomena*, § 87.
86. *Prolegomena*, § 91.
87. F. H. Bradley, *Ethical Studies*, 177.
88. B. Bosanquet, *Philosophical Theory of the State* (London, 1965; originally published 1899) xlvii (Introduction to the 3rd edition 1920).
89. Ibid. xxxiii.
90. Ibid. 178–9.
91. *PR* § 137.